GAP YEAR

GAP YEAR

How Delaying College Changes People in Ways the World Needs

JOSEPH O'SHEA

Johns Hopkins University Press

BALTIMORE

© 2014 Johns Hopkins University Press
All rights reserved. Published 2014
Printed in the United States of America on acid-free paper

9 8 7 6 5 4 3 2 1

Johns Hopkins University Press
2715 North Charles Street
Baltimore, Maryland 21218-4363
www.press.jhu.edu

Library of Congress Cataloging-in-Publication Data

O'Shea, Joseph, 1986–
    Gap year : how delaying college changes people in ways the world
needs / Joseph O'Shea.
        p.   cm.
    Includes bibliographical references and index.
    ISBN 978-1-4214-1036-4 (pbk.) — ISBN 978-1-4214-1037-1
(electronic) — ISBN 1-4214-1036-2 (pbk.) 1. Gap years. 2. Non-
formal education. 3. Experiential learning. 4. High school graduates—
Life skills guides. I. Title.
    LC45.3.O75 2013
    378.1'98—dc23   2013012252

A catalog record for this book is available from the British Library.

*Special discounts are available for bulk purchases of this book. For
more information, please contact Special Sales at 410-516-6936 or
specialsales@press.jhu.edu.*

Johns Hopkins University Press uses environmentally friendly book
materials, including recycled text paper that is composed of at least
30 percent post-consumer waste, whenever possible.

In memory of my parents, Jim and Debbie O'Shea

Contents

Preface

I began this book after a period of great change in my life. My parents had both recently died, and I was trying to reconstitute my identity without them. I was growing increasingly reflective about my own life and development. I became motivated to understand how we come to be the people we are—and what society can do to influence that path for a young person. My own personal quest for identity and character development ultimately gave rise to an academic interest in how students mature in what was then my new home, the United Kingdom. When I looked at the higher education environment in that country, I encountered a very interesting phenomenon that had not yet taken hold in my home country, the United States: the well-established precollege gap year.

This book is the product of my journey to explore and better understand these gap years. I feel fortunate to have had this opportunity to study education and human development, which are so central to our lives and have dominated my reflections on my own life. Indeed, the struggles I faced in capturing the experiences of participants in this study reflect some of my own difficulties understanding the complex and interrelated influences on me as a young person. Despite these obstacles, investigating this topic has helped shed some light on my journey in life. I hope this book contributes, in small part, to our understanding both of gap years and of how we come to be the people we are.

This book would not have been possible without the generous support and feedback I received from numerous friends, colleagues, and teachers, especially David Mills, Ben Eidelson, and Sherif Girgis. Thanks to the Rhodes Trust, which funded the studies out of which this project grew. I am also grateful to Project Trust and the participants in this study. Finally, I thank my family and my partner for their incredible patience and encouragement.

GAP YEAR

Introduction

The challenges of our time demand an educational system that can help young people to become citizens of the world. We need our students to be smart, critical, and innovative thinkers but also people of character who use their talents to help others.

Coming up with such a system is difficult, especially because human development is so complex and multifaceted. But one principal lesson from educational and psychological research is clear: We often develop most when our understandings of ourselves and the world around us are challenged—when we engage with people and ideas that are different. Despite this insight, we often prioritize comfort and self-segregate into groups of sameness. We tend to surround ourselves with people who think, talk, and look similar to us. So how do we encourage young people to engage with difference in ways that catalyze their development?

Traditionally, the U.S. higher education system has championed the idea of liberal arts education as a means to engage students with difference, to expand their worldview beyond their known universe. Harvard University's Committee on General Education highlights this approach:

> The aim of a liberal education is to unsettle presumptions, to defamiliarize the familiar, to reveal what is going on beneath and behind appearances, to disorient young people and to help them to find ways to re-orient themselves. A liberal education aims to accomplish these things by questioning assumptions, by inducing self-reflection . . . by encounters with radically different historical moments and cultural formations. (Harvard University 2007, 1–2)

However, formal classroom education alone cannot accomplish this aim. The classroom is limited in its ability to engage students with difference and contribute to their development as able citizens. We also need experiential influences and critical self-reflection to cultivate our dispositions and moral sentiments.

Taking a gap year—in which people delay college for a year and live and volunteer in communities radically different from their own—is one promising approach to supplementing formal education. Although the rising popularity of the gap year in the United Kingdom, the United States, Australia, and elsewhere has sparked a debate about its benefits, little research has been done to examine these effects.

In this book I argue that gap years can be a powerful educational experience. They can contribute to growth in how young adults make meaning of themselves, their relationships, and the world around them such that they develop capacities and perspectives for effective citizenship.

The Rise of the Gap Year

The gap year developed from the British experience. Scholars suggest that the European Grand Tour was the historical precursor to the modern gap year (Heath 2007; King 2007; Simpson 2004). During the late seventeenth to the early nineteenth centuries, the Grand Tour was a form of travel for young British aristocratic men to explore art, history, and culture in Europe. It served as an extended educational experience: "the travel [practice] of a young man of rank often in his teen, undertaken as the 'crown' of his liberal education" (Cohen 2001, 129). Scholars also argue that the legacy of the British Empire and the hippie trail of countercultural youth who traveled the world in the 1960s and early 1970s have contributed to the growth of the modern gap year (Heath 2007, 100; Simpson 2004).

Gap years have been become more common in recent years. For instance, in 1986 in the United Kingdom, only an estimated 5.5 percent of college applicants took a "year out" before college (Ansell 2008). However, of the 391,000 people with an accepted application to a UK university in 2006, it is estimated that about 45,000 to 50,000 (12–13 percent) had taken or would take (through deferred admission) a gap year (Ansell 2008; Heath 2007; University and Colleges Admissions Service 2006). Gap years have also become increasingly common in Australia. It was estimated that in 1974 only about 4 percent of students took a gap year, but by 2004 the proportion had risen to 11 percent (Birch and Miller 2007). The practice has even spread to Japan, with some universities encouraging their students to take a gap year (Ito 2011).

Although there are no comprehensive statistics regarding gap year participation in the United States, the practice seems to be catching on there as well. Robert Clagett, a former dean of admissions at Middlebury College and former senior admissions officer at Harvard College, recently observed: "More and more students are stepping off the educational treadmill, pursuing interests and reminding themselves in the process of what their education is really all about" (Clagett 2011). Among U.S. higher education institutions, Harvard has the longest tradition of encouraging students to take a gap year before matriculation, a position it has held for more than 30 years. Harvard saw a 33 percent jump in the number of students taking gap years in the past decade (Gregory 2010). In 2009, Princeton University launched a subsidized international volunteering gap year option for incoming students with the hope that 10 percent of the student body would participate in coming years (Arenson 2008). In September 2012, the New School, a university in New York City, announced that students who take an international volunteering gap year with their partner organization will earn 30 academic credits for the experience and start at the university as sophomores (Chafin 2012). A growing number of directors of admissions at public universities, such as the University of South Carolina and the University of California–Santa Barbara, have also reported an increase in gap year students and accommodate them through a special deferral process.

There is also an emerging industry of gap year providers in the United States. These organizations offer structured gap year programs for students, curating the experience by helping place students in their gap year roles and supporting them during the year. Global Citizen Year is among the most prominent, aiming to develop a network of promising leaders though a gap year of international service. These providers, under the banner of USA Gap Year Fairs, now hold a circuit of events across the United States annually to promote the experience (Cheng and Pendoley 2012).

While many young people spend their gap year working domestically or travelling independently, others volunteer internationally in an estimated 200 countries through more than 800 organizations (Jones 2005). In this book, I primarily discuss the precollege international volunteering gap year—what has been called the original form of the gap year and what Sue Heath deemed the "gold standard" of gap years (2007).

According to Nicola Ansell, there has been a "dramatic expansion" of structured gap year volunteer placements in the developing world (2008, 7). Referring to overseas volunteer opportunities more generally, including those outside the gap year context, Andrew Jones (2004) estimates that about 350,000 overseas volunteering placements—often called projects—are offered annually to people aged 16–25, with a large share taken up by UK- and U.S.-based participants. Most placements in the developing world last 3–12 months, with an estimated 45 percent of overseas placements in social and community work (including health care and teaching), 21 percent involving work with children (often in orphanages), 17 percent involving conservation/environmental work, and 12 percent involving construction projects (Jones 2004). During the course of the year, volunteers occasionally supplement these placements by creating their own small-scale secondary projects, such as after-school programs or community gardens (see chapter 2).

Structured, international volunteering gap year programs range in price, with some costing less than $3,000 and others more $20,000, depending on a number of factors, such as flights, organizational support from the provider organization, insurance, and room and board for a year. Living in a developing country can be relatively inexpensive, however, and many gap year volunteers live with a local host family. Some gap year providers are able to offer lower cost options by subsidizing the volunteers' costs with funding from grants or even the developing country's government. Students themselves often fundraise to help pay for the gap year by appealing to family, friends, and community organizations; by hosting events like cook-offs and car washes; and through online means like crowdfunding websites.

Despite its increased popularity, international gap year opportunities are thought to be distributed unevenly among the population, specifically concentrated among the middle and upper classes. Heath, a sociologist of education, sees this distribution as a source of concern, criticizing gap years—especially the international volunteering gap year—for providing unequal advantages to those who can and do take them. She argues that the gap year's popularity is largely the result of motivations to gain a competitive advantage (e.g., in cultural capital) over other applicants in an increasingly competitive marketplace and higher education system. Heath (2007, 101) writes:

> It is no coincidence that the gap year's popularity has taken off in parallel with this expansion, as taking the "right" sort of year out is emerging as an important means of gaining distinction over peers. In a period of increased competition and heightened emphasis on the "economy of experience," the gap year serves to widen the gap between different groups of students as part of an ongoing process of positional competition.

A Gap Year Debate

Criticism of the gap year has mounted in recent years as well, which is itself a testament to the emergence of the practice as an established institution. In particular, a debate has arisen regarding the impact these experiences can have on the people who undertake them and whether these experiences should be financially supported (e.g., with government resources or by higher education institutions).

Providers often claim that the year can be life-changing and that it can help create better prepared and more highly motivated students in a short period of time (Blackburn, Clark, and Pilgrim 2005). In a summary of gap year providers' claims, Heath (2007) outlines a number of promised benefits: acquiring soft skills (such as better organization and communication), personal development, self-reflection and career clarification, a better adaptation to college life, and greater attractiveness to employers.

People have been finding fault with this form of educational experience since the days of the Grand Tour. One eighteenth-century critic said: "The tour of Europe is a paltry thing . . . a uniform, unvaried prospect" that served to reinforce old preconceptions and prejudices about national characteristics (Bohls and Duncan 2005, 19). Philosopher Adam Smith wrote in 1776 in *The Wealth of Nations*:

> In England, it becomes every day more and more the custom to send young people to travel in foreign countries immediately upon their leaving school, and without sending them to any university . . . By travelling so very young, by spending in the most frivolous dissipation the most precious years of his life . . . every useful habit, which the earlier parts of his education might have had some tendency to form in him, instead of being riveted and confirmed, is almost necessarily either weakened or effaced. Nothing but the discredit into which the universities are allowing themselves to fall, could ever have brought into repute so very absurd a practice as that of travelling at this early period of life. (Smith 1776/1976, 773–774)

Andrew Jones (2004) and Sue Heath (2007) highlight the emerging debate over the value of modern gap year experiences, notably overseas volunteering gap years, for people who take them. There is growing negativity toward gap years in the popular media, questioning both what young people get out of a year and whether what they do during their year has value for others. In line with this general criticism, the chief executive of the United Kingdom's Universities and College Admissions Service (UCAS) declared in 2010 that the "golden age of the gap year is over" and that high school graduates should instead concentrate on getting work experience and extra training before starting their degrees (Barrett 2010). In a piece in the United Kingdom's *Guardian* newspaper, commentator David Mitchell wrote: "Gap-year travel may broaden the mind—but who needs a broad mind these days? Youngsters should buckle down rather than gadding around the world before going to university" (2011). Numerous newspaper articles in the United Kingdom have suggested that the gap year is a waste at best and a hypocritical indulgence at worst.

Universities sometimes adopt a dismissive attitude toward gap years as well. Trinity College in Cambridge, for example, tells prospective math students: "We are also willing to consider applications from those seeking to defer entry for a year, although it is felt that deferred entry is not generally beneficial for those wishing to study mathematics." However, some universities, such as the University of Leeds, formally support the gap year, if the year is spent doing something "productive": thus "deferred entry is encouraged for those applicants who wish to spend a year gaining experience of work, voluntary service or travel." One explanation of these different attitudes is that the colleges and universities that formally discourage gap years are more narrowly interested in the cognitive capacities of their potential students. As an admission tutor at the University of Oxford explained to me:

> I don't think students will have any better chance of getting in because of a gap year, though it may allow them to explore their subject in more depth, which is always welcome. We don't take extra-curricular activities into account during admissions anyway, so unless they do something related to the course they're applying for, it won't make a difference to their application.

The value that students who take gap years bring to an academic institution is not the only thing being called into question. Some writers have also criticized the gap year options available to young people as being relatively poorly organized, under-resourced, and lacking quality assurance (Simpson 2004). The debate over the gap year has spilled over into public policy discussions, where many disagree as to whether the growth of these programs and the organizations involved in providing placements should be supported by government policies and resources. This debate has become more salient recently as increases in tuition fees threaten to deter high school graduates from taking gap year placements. The UK government, however, has actively supported gap years in the past, and a minister was made specifically responsible for gap years in 2002 (*Guardian* 2002).

At the same time as there is increasingly negative press in the United Kingdom, there is growing and largely positive attention paid to gap years in the United States. *Time* magazine recently published a story that featured students who had taken a gap year offering glowing reviews of their experiences (Gregory 2010). Nicholas Kristof, a *New York Times* columnist whose son took a gap year in China, is an advocate of gap years as well. In a recent piece, he wrote, "If you're a high school senior, think about taking a 'gap year'—nearly all colleges will defer admission—and exploring the world. It'll be cheaper than a year of college and may well be more educational" (Kristof 2010).

The Need for Research

Although gap years have gained in popularity, their efficacy is unclear. In this book, I situate that debate in a broader framework. How do gap years actually act pedagogically to help people learn, what role do they play in a person's development, and how do they fit into the discussion of making meaning out of life and indeed help people become full members of civic society?

Despite the cultural prominence of the gap year and the emerging debate regarding its merits, there has been little empirical research on the subject regarding any of these broader questions. Much of the existing research is on the gap year industry itself and comes from an international development perspective that criticizes the industry for its limited impact on poverty and for the ways it portrays the developing world. A small amount of research, largely from a sociological perspective, examines the gap year in light of modernizing and postmodern trends in society. Some studies have looked at the academic performance of gap year students while in college. In Australia and the United Kingdom, economic researchers found that high school students who deferred their admission to college to take a gap year went to college (after their gap year) at the same rate as those who accepted an offer and intended to go straight there (Birch and Miller 2007; Crawford and Cribb 2012). They also found that taking a gap year had a significant positive impact on students' academic performance in college, with the strongest impact for students who had applied to college with grades on the lower end of the distribution (Birch and Miller 2007; Crawford and Cribb 2012). In fact, in the United Kingdom, students who had taken a gap year were more likely to graduate with higher grade point averages than observationally identical individuals who went straight to college, and this effect was seen even for gap year students with lower academic achievement in high school (Crawford and Cribb 2012). Similarly, from a survey of 338 college students in Australia, psychologist Andrew Martin found that students who participated in a gap year had higher levels of academic motivation than did those who went straight to college, even when controlling for demographic factors, hypothesizing that "a gap year may be one means of addressing motivational difficulties that might have been present at school" (Martin 2010, 572). At Middlebury College in Vermont, internal research found that gap year students had higher GPAs and held a disproportionate number of leadership positions on campus than did their non–gap year counterparts, even when controlling for high school academic backgrounds (Buckles 2013; Clagett 2011).

Research specifically on the international volunteering gap year has been conducted only with shorter-term experiences and suggests broadly that the international volunteering gap year can have benefits in personal development and learning (Jones 2004). However, there is little consensus on this point, as Kate Simpson (2004) argues that the learning is limited and simplistic. At most, there is a loose and tangled set of assumptions about what this type of gap year provides—or does not provide—for the people who participate. As Heath (2007, 100) points out:

> In the absence of much existing academic research on the gap year, many of the claims of the gap-year industry concerning the presumed benefits of taking a year out are based on perceptions rather than on solid evidence. There is, therefore, a clear need for systematic research into the gap year and its impact on students.

The Dual Aims of This Book

In this book, I hope to fill in at least a few of the deficits in this research. In an effort to do so, I have divided the book into two parts. In the first part, I relay stories people told about their gap years. Through these narratives, I show how volunteers understand their experiences to have affected their relationships with others, their perceptions of themselves, and their views of the world at large. Each chapter in this part concludes with analysis into how participants' experiences fit with current theory on education and the psychology of development.

Most of the data for this section of the book came from participants who took part in a gap year through a prominent UK-based, international gap year provider organization, Project Trust. Established in 1967, it is the oldest gap year organization in existence. The organization offers yearlong international volunteering gap year placements for secondary school graduates. During their gap year, these participants (who were mostly middle class) were spread among Central and South America, the Caribbean, sub-Saharan Africa, and Asia. Students were typically placed at a volunteering project in pairs and lived in various types of accommodations (such as with a local family, in a room at their workplace, or in their own small house or apartment). The students most often volunteered as teachers, but many also worked in other community placements such as nonprofit orphanages, day care centers, or even newspapers and outdoor education centers.

To get the narratives for this book, I used three sources. First, I drew on participant observation and interviews with nearly 180 students before and shortly after gap year experiences, paying particular attention to students who seemed to have negative or extremely influential experiences over the year. Second, I conducted in-depth, 1–3 hour interviews with 31 students who had completed their gap years and were currently in college. These students ranged from first to final year college students, and I traveled to meet them at the universities where they currently studied, at their homes, or elsewhere. Third, I analyzed more than 400 gap year students' end-of-year reports. To supplement this data, I also interviewed a dozen parents of gap year volunteers and eight staff members of gap year provider organizations.

In the second part of the book, I help make sense of these stories by situating them in educational, psychological, and philosophical theories of thinkers such as Plato, John Dewey, Robert Kegan, and Paolo Freire. I illustrate how the year contributed to growth in both participants' personal and public lives. First, I show how the year not only served to develop *how* participants think—the processes through which they come to understand the world—but also changed *what* they think—the particular meanings they make of themselves, others, and world around them. I then examine the implications of these changes and argue that the gap year promoted participants' development as cosmopolitan citizens and community members, enriching what I refer to as their civic meaning-making. In the last chapter, I show how the experiences detailed in the narratives and the theories of education and human development can aid in creating and designing a gap year that helps change people in ways the world needs.

Part I / **Experiencing the Gap Year**

1

Reasons for Taking a Year

Why do students decided to leave their families, their communities, and their countries to go live and volunteer for a year in a developing country often thousands of miles away from home? In this chapter, I examine the various motivations behind these students' decisions to take a gap year and their motivations to stay and continue their work during the year. Despite my presentation of these motivations as separated, they are overlapping and occur in different combinations for each participant.

In deciding to undertake the gap year, students reported a combination of motives. However, contrary to many industry appeals to altruism, students tended to have largely egoistic motivations for undertaking their international volunteering gap year. As one said, "No volunteer goes only for the altruism—to help the country."

To be sure, volunteers did have some altruistic aims in their decisions to take the year. One shared how "idea of helping others really appealed to [her]," while another who spent her year in China recalled that she "had an idealism to help" the people there. Others wanted to "make a difference in the world," while a few also expressed a concept about fairness, as one volunteer said: "I see people on TV . . . and I want to help them. They don't deserve that, and I want to help."

Despite these altruistic motives, students principally intended to use the experience to obtain a variety of perceived benefits. Often they wanted to use the gap year to develop skills, perspectives, and traits that they felt they lacked and had not developed in school or their home communities.

Off the Beaten Track

Fundamentally, these students sought out something "different" and "new." They longed for something more; often their desires were vague and ambiguous, but they were motivated by an unsatisfied curiosity about the world—to see what else is out there—and a desire to "get out" from their hometowns. Students reported using the gap year as a way out of a "bubble" or "sheltered life." Abigail highlighted this: "Everyone is just so comfortable in my town; my parents . . . no one leaves. I want to get out and see what else is there." Erik felt a similar desire before his gap year: "I am bored and confined to the same things. I want to get away from this controlled environment; there is not enough to do. I want to get out and adventure and experience more."

By leaving their hometowns, students hoped to experience other ways of living. For instance, one said: "I want to experience life and diversity, and see how people live without material possessions." They thought these new ways of living would change the way they look at the world, as one student said: "The gap year is a very personal experience—I am doing this for me—to get a new perspective on Scotland and the world." Some students, away from their home social pressures, thought they could be *freer* to act during their gap year: "I want to do things I love, and I have always held back—but I won't hold back there."

Many also expressed a resistance to the "academic treadmill" or current pressures on youth, using the gap year as a means to buck the traditional path. Samantha declared: "I want to break out from education; I don't need to follow the track." Others said: "I felt jaded by school after 13 years . . . I needed a break"; and "I have been part of an education factory for so long—I just want to get out—do and see something completely different—something really alien." Some students specifically wanted to use the gap year as a means to be countercultural and express to society that they did not want or have to follow the traditional trajectory: one said she wanted to do the gap year to be "unique," while another recalled, "I wanted to stick it to the man."

Many of the students' motivations for a gap year reflected disenchantment with the school system, stemming from what they saw as a "narrow" focus in schools, a perceived academic detachment from "practical things" or the "real world," or the length of the schooling process without a break. One student said: "The focus in school is too narrow; they just care about exams, not me as a person." Another recalled: "I didn't want to work for just another grade. I wanted to do something that had an impact right when I was doing it." Students felt they wanted to develop in ways outside of academics: "I want to learn things that I can't learn at university"; "My brain is saturated with useless information . . . I am ready for information that I will need"; and "I want to learn things that I didn't learn in school, like independence, dealing with problems, fixing things, and organizational skills." Another shared that since she saw college principally as vocational training, she wanted to use the gap year to do "something more" than just train for a job.

Students often wanted to use their gap year to learn about themselves in new ways, as Ingrid reported: "I want to figure out who I am independent of my parents and community." In a similar vein, students sometimes hoped the year would help them figure out what they wanted to do in life—they expressed indecision about their future and the pressure to choose a career trajectory at an early age. As one gap year participant explained: "There was so much pressure to choose a career so early in life. I felt I didn't know what I wanted to do, so I did a gap year." Echoing this, others said: "I want to use the year to figure out if I want to go to university"; "The year will help me find out who I am and what I am interested in; maybe I do not want to do law—I don't want to make a mistake on what to do." Some students thought the year could be used to try out a vocational direction before embarking on a college degree in the field, as one student, Henry, reported, "I am here to try new things . . . to see if [teaching] is what I want to do in life."

Out of the Comfort Zone

Some students wanted to use the gap year (often their first extended period away from family) to challenge or test themselves in ways that they felt would help them to develop or learn about themselves and others. Students said the gap year was a response to a desire to "do something on my own," to "accomplish something without much help from others," or do be "independent." Another student expressed: "I want to really challenge myself; I want to cry and really be challenged. You get everything so easy today—your parents do everything, and it's so easy to go to university. I want to work for something; I want to struggle and work." Some thought that living a different way of life during their year provided this challenge: "I definitely have the motivation to experience both life with the less fortunate and international development, principally because I think it will be really challenging, and completely contrary to my thus far sheltered, middle-class, rural upbringing." It is interesting to note that some students shared that the challenge of a "hard-core" option of full year gap year was what attracted them. As one gap year participant said, "I wanted more than 3 months. I really wanted to push myself."

In seeking out these gap year challenges and experiences, students reported that they hoped to use the year for personal and sometimes interpersonal development. They wanted a time of accelerated personal growth and, for some, to use the gap year as a rite of passage into adulthood. Mark highlighted this, saying: "I am naive about the world. I want to become a man; I want to take responsibility, to do and plan something myself, something that can fail." Others thought the gap year would help them to develop traits such as greater "confidence," "social skills," "independence," or to become "more extroverted." Tobias, a student who went to Chile, said: "I wasn't sure how I wanted to change from my gap year—I just thought change would be good . . . I didn't like going out [back home]—I just thought that going out in Chile would be different. I wanted to have to do things I wouldn't do, I wanted to become more extroverted . . . I wanted to be forced to be brave." A potential volunteer, who was ultimately not selected to take a gap year with a provider (largely due to mental health reasons), said: "The message I am getting at school is that I am not a good leader, so I want to use the experience to improve. I want an experience to help in university, to develop people skills, to be able to talk to people."

Getting Ready for College

Students often also reported using the gap year to delay college; they were "not ready to go to university" yet or "don't want to go straight through." Typically, they felt that it was important to acquire new skills and perspectives before heading to college; one, for example, expressed that he wanted to be "more equipped" before he matriculates. A few volunteers reported they were steered toward a gap year because they did not gain admission to a university, as one said: "I did a gap year because my grades were not good enough to get into university, and I didn't want to start working right away." This approach was at times successful, with some volunteers reporting that their marks were not high enough to get into a specific university. For example, Kyle said, "Because I was doing this gap year they let me in."

Immersion in a New Culture

Most students sought out this particular type of gap year (of a long duration and with volunteering as the primary activity) to become immersed in a new community. They expressed a desire to get a more in-depth perspective on a community, to experience and learn about another language and culture, and to get the chance to know a local community. One student said: "I have a narrow view of the world . . . I want to feel what it is really like to live in another country . . . to stay a long time and volunteer there." Others wanted to distance themselves from tourists by becoming immersed: "I was on a holiday, and a group of Japanese tourists came off their bus with their cameras glued to their faces; the way they treated the community . . . I didn't like it." Some participants were motivated to take an international volunteering gap year because of a curiosity about life in poverty or specific aspects about a particular country's politics or culture. Tim, for example, cited his desire to learn about the life of the less fortunate and the politics of China.

Being Part of a Community

Although these gap year students saw volunteering as a way to help others, many also viewed it as a means of integration into the community and a medium for learning about the culture. For instance, one participant said he wanted to volunteer because "you get more out of it when you volunteer because you can be more accepted into the community." Another student expressed his curiosity and desire to help: "I want to experience poverty rather than watching it on TV. And I want to help; I want to make a difference and do my part, at least it will make me feel good for a few years while I do law." Others thought that their role as a volunteer and a "professional" working in the community—and living in much the same conditions as local people—would help them be accepted by local people.

Also, because students felt they were going to personally gain from a gap year, they often wanted to give something to the community in return. Aaron, for example, felt volunteering was a way for him to "give something back while learning." Others were skeptical about volunteering and its impacts on the community before their year, but reasoned that by spending a year there they had a greater chance of making a difference than with a shorter term program; one student expressed his desire for a yearlong program with this: "I want to help people properly."

Getting Away from Problems

For some students the year was motivated by a desire to "escape" from a home environment or family. One said: "This is a way for me to get away from all my problems at home." Another student, Anjali, shared: "I am always trying to please my dad; nothing is good enough for him. But during a gap year, I won't have to please him because he won't be there, and I will be away from family and people who want me to be something."

Others wanted to use the year to address personal problems or "fix" mental health disorders (e.g., depression, eating disorders). One student with an eating disorder said before her year: "The gap year is the only light I can see out of this tunnel." A gap year participant who said he was depressed before his year reflected: "I needed a change, and the gap year was a way to change everything." In another example, a student who said she was diagnosed with depression expressed this before her year: "This is a chance to start off fresh; to get away; to go to a place that no one will know me. My mom thinks I am just trying to get away from everything and my problems, but I see it as going towards something, something that I need to help me. I am making the best choice for me."

Some other students with mental health disorders believed a gap year would help them to see the world differently. Jonathon described his future gap year almost as a treatment for his clinical depression: "The gap year could really help me. This is a way to help myself, to develop myself to get over problems." He said that he wanted to go to China during his year to help change his view of the world: "It is so different; it would give me a different way to see the world." Jonathon wanted to prove to others that he could overcome the challenge of the gap year and that he was "better": "I want to prove to others that I am strong enough to do this."

Some students with more severe or ongoing mental disorders were not selected to take a gap year with the sponsoring organization. Likewise, some students with the greatest, and perhaps unrealistic, expectations of how the gap year could solve their problems were not selected. For instance, one student who was rejected said she "feels all alone in the world" and that the year would help her to "grow and mature as a person" and find "meaning in life." She expressed that a gap year was the "best thing for me and that it will help me the most." The fact that gap year organizations sometimes reject these students reflects how mental health issues can often be dangerous overseas and highlights the worries of using the gap year as a "treatment," a topic that will be explored further in the next chapter. In addition, candidates with very high and specific expectations about the year were often volunteers who had difficulty adjusting to the new environment, as reality did not meet expectations overseas, contributing to some leaving their gap year early.

The Time Was Right

Both before and after their gap year, students believed that the best time in their lives to take a gap year was before college. Many felt that they were more malleable at a young age and that a precollege gap year would have maximum impact on them and their future. Luke heighted this: "At this age, you can still be very open; you can still question things and how you will define your way of life and personality." In addition, some students wanted to do a gap year before college partly because they "felt young for [their] year in school" and wanted to be the same age as the other first year students. Also, students believed that the year was a "once in a lifetime" or "rare opportunity"; that they would not have another time in their lives with as little responsibilities or commitments (such as family or career) or a time when it was more socially acceptable to take a gap year. Many also felt that a postcollege gap year would be difficult, citing that after college their career path would be "set" and that student loan repayment would prevent taking time out of paid work.

Long-Term Benefits

Students also felt the skills they would gain during their gap year would help them in the long term. They thought the year would allow them to "get the most out of university" from being more mature before starting, as well as having more solidified interests. Some students also believed the year would help them learn how to interact with a greater range of people, which would benefit them in college. Many also thought the break from academic study would "recharge their batteries" or help them be more "motivated" in education. Before his year, James proclaimed, "I will bounce back from it and be really ready for intellectual study again after a year of growing up."

Although it was not a primary motivation, a few participants reported that they believed the year would help them with their career, enhancing their CV for employers or college admissions. While some believed that the "life skills" or experiences would help them in any career, others wanted to gain skills specific to their major area or career (e.g., learn a language for their degree in international relations) as well as to compensate for skills they felt were lacking before heading on the job market.

Family Attitudes

Students reported varying levels of family support for their decision to take a gap year. Some described how their parents "really liked the idea of a gap year" and saw many benefits for their child. In fact, some students said that their parents "pushed" them to do the year. Similarly, sometimes a parent or sibling had taken a gap year, which made volunteers feel pressure to take one themselves. One gap year volunteer, for instance, whose two siblings had done gap years, said: "It wasn't even a question if I was going to do a gap year; it was just what is done in our family." Sometimes, students felt that their parents used the experience to live vicariously through them: "My mom really like the idea of a gap year but never took one. I am reliving her dream; she is vicariously living through my experiences." However, some reported that their parents did not support their taking a gap year. These students, who seemed to come largely from working-class backgrounds, said their parents did not "understand" why they wanted to do it or felt that they should go directly to college or, more commonly, directly into a career.

Interviews conducted at a gap year provider's parents' meetings suggest that, despite some reservations, most parents of these gap year students reported being supportive of their child's taking a year out—often helping him or her in fundraising and preparing for the year. Parents often believed the year would be beneficial for their child and that it would help develop qualities and traits that they wanted to (and have been trying to) instill in them. One parent highlighted that she hoped the year developed in her daughter "more appreciation and a sense of what she has and the life she leads, and what we do for her"; while others hoped the year would teach their child to "not [take] things for granted," develop a "selfless attitude," a more "worldly perspective," or "independence." One father wanted his son to use the year to "grow up and come back as a man." Sometimes, parents reported that they had traveled or had taken a gap year themselves when they were young, believing that the time served them well, while others said it was a chance from them to live vicariously through their child and do something they always wanted to do but could not.

Changing Motivations during the Year

Throughout the experience, volunteers' narratives suggest that a combination of both altruistic and egoistic motives was critical to their investing in the gap year, sacrificing during the year, and overcoming hardships. Confronting a realization of their limited impact of their volunteering efforts, participants often reminded themselves that they were not only there to help others but to develop themselves and to have an "experience."

Once the students got into their gap year, however, their motivations to stay—and often to invest themselves in the project—often seemed to have had a more others-centered component. This altruism reflected a growing concern for those around them and in their care. In fact, participants articulated a number of instances where they thought about leaving but did not, often because they felt the children in their care or others needed them. One said: "I was never going to leave or give up as I could never do that to the children." Carla, a volunteer in Peru, highlighted how the children in her care were the reason she stayed and overcame the "office politics" and challenges during her year: "It was difficult to act professionally when our work was being disregarded as unimportant by the Director . . . but over the year I really learned to just focus on what is most important—the kids. I learned to carry on, motivate myself and put as much effort into my work as possible, so that it could be appreciated by the kids, whom we were really there for."

For many participants becoming integrated into and feeling part of the community was also motivation to stay and invest themselves—to work, learn the local language, build relationships, to take part in and give to the community. Feeling part of the community—which typically developed after several months for volunteers—was a particularly powerful motivation and highly regarded reward. One described it as a pleasure of changing an "unfamiliar place to your home." Adding to this, volunteers expressed a growing appreciation for their opportunity to be part of the gap year community and what the community has provided them, motivating many to "give back" more. For example, one said: "Feeling part of the community, and knowing that you have changed and made it as part of the community—you feel grateful and want to give back and help others . . . it pushes you to give to others." Another volunteer recalled: "They were giving so much to me, I felt like I couldn't give back enough." However, this desire to give to others and the community was often influenced by the role volunteers had and the organizational culture in which they were operating (e.g., if volunteers did not feel valued or needed in their role, it affected their commitment). These mitigating dynamics will be discussed further in the final chapter on designing the gap year.

Not Letting People Down

Volunteers also reported that their fundraising efforts before the year (to help pay for the gap year program fees) created another obstacle to leaving early. Leaving early would "let down" or "disappoint" the donors who helped them to take their gap year. Similarly, they did not want to "let down" those in their gap year community overseas, the gap year provider, or their volunteering partner. As one volunteer said, "Sometimes I felt that I was not appreciated there and I thought about leaving, but I didn't leave because I didn't want to let everyone down—my partner, the school—I felt needed even if the school didn't think I was." Many volunteers were also partly motivated by a personal "pride" and desire to "stick it out" to accomplish the goal and finish the year. Support from people in the volunteer's life (e.g., a volunteer partner, local people, family, gap year provider staff, etc.) gave volunteers a reason beyond their personal motivations to participate in the gap year and provided a powerful impetus to overcome struggles during the year.

Analysis

This chapter explored the motivations of gap year participants and their conceptions of what their experiences will be like. Fundamentally, students conceived of the year in various ways as an instrument of change. This suggests that the students are positioning themselves to be engaged in the experience and challenged in new ways (often to try and "get the most out of" a "once in a lifetime opportunity"). In other words, it suggests that students were becoming "ready" for the possible changes that could occur (Sanford 1962). Nevitt Sanford outlines this concept of readiness in learners: "What the state of readiness means most essentially is that the individual is now open to new kinds of stimuli and prepared to deal with them in an adaptive way" (1962, 257).

The readiness of gap year volunteers may be an important factor in the process of changing the ways they understand the world, as volunteers may be more receptive to changes and influences. As one said, "I didn't know how it was going to change me; I just thought change would be good." To be sure, while the gap year is often a very positive experience for volunteers, there may be some selection effect occurring. That is, the people who take these gap years are precisely those who are looking to change. That said, it is important to emphasize that volunteers stated that they did not expect many of the changes that ensued from the year.

Examining volunteers' motivations also reveals an interesting relationship, one contrary to Sue Heath's (2007) argument concerning the gap year's popularity. Heath suggests that the gap year's rise is largely the result of motivations by participants to gain an advantage over other applicants in an increasingly competitive marketplace and higher education system. However, her hypothesis does not sit well with responses in my research. In fact, many volunteers were actually motivated by a *rejection* of this system of increasing competition and script for young people's lives. Students often were motivated to "get out" of formal education, the "academic treadmill," and a "narrow" focus on career preparation in the education system and society—to "break free" as one student put it.

In addition, despite many gap year industry appeals to altruism, I found largely egoistic motivations present in deciding to take the year. That participants wanted to use volunteering largely to develop themselves—and often in ways they felt their school did not offer them—reflects Louis Zurcher's idea of the compensatory function of volunteer work (1978) and supports Robert Serow's (1991) hypothesis that students often use volunteering to compensate for the lack of concrete experience and skill development from their schooling. This is also in line with other research that described volunteer motives as an altruism–egoism mixture—with different combinations of motivations for each person (Brooks 2002; Hustinx 2001; Yeung 2004). However, I found that there seems to be convergence of motivations for volunteers during the year toward a growing importance of altruistic endeavors; many volunteers reported staying on and continuing their work until the end of their placement for the benefit of the people in their care. In other words, volunteers often described moving to a more others-focused orientation during the year, and this seemed, as discussed later in this book, to continue after their return.

It is important to consider, as Ruth Unstead-Joss (2008, 18) suggests, how the "context itself influences motivation." For instance, how the gap year organization communicated and marketed the experience seemed to affect the dispositions of volunteers. The gap year provider Project Trust tells its participants how "challenging" and "intense" the experience is and that participants will "change" from their participation. Cultural connotations associated with a gap year—and the "challenge" and potential for change that they signal—often seemed to contribute to volunteers' thinking about their motivations and their experiences ahead in those ways. In addition, programmatic messaging seemed to help temper and direct the expectations and energies of future volunteers, such as the gap year provider's explicit aim for volunteers to integrate into the community. A mismatch of expectations and reality often led to frustrations, as one volunteer highlighted: "I thought it would be African, like mud huts, but it wasn't; I was disappointed it wasn't more different when I arrived."

Together, these findings help to build an initial empirical grounding of the study of participant motivations in an international volunteering gap year. Specifically, they begin to outline the various motivations and their dynamics that can occur before and during these types of gap years, an aspect of the gap year that has been greatly under-researched.

2

Changes in Themselves

Gap year volunteers nearly universally commented on the profound, often life-altering impact they felt the experience had on their lives. As a volunteer teacher in rural Honduras said, "As cliché as it sounds, it was life changing. It changes the way you look at the world and the way you look at yourself." Although the perceived outcomes of taking a gap year are different for each person, there are some clear patterns and themes.

Understanding of Themselves

Participants frequently recalled how the gap year helped them "understand themselves" and become more "comfortable" with whom they are as distinct people and less susceptible to the "pressures" of others. Carla, a volunteer in Peru, illustrated this: "It sounds strange, but I also feel a lot calmer and content with myself than I did before." Other volunteers expressed this theme:

> Before I went on my gap year, I was very influenced by what other people said and did; since then I am more certain in my personality and decision making abilities. —*Florence*, South Africa

> I don't need to seek approval of others as much; I am more comfortable with myself. —*Samantha*, Honduras

> I feel that I am much more aware of who I am now. —*Jason*, Botswana

Highlighting this same theme, Brenda, a volunteer in Honduras, emphasized the great intrapersonal learning and changes she felt she underwent. She described her year as more "challenging than fun" and said: "I realized that I can be what I want to be. Before I was the person that my parents wanted me to be, but I realized I have my own personality and my own views. No one is pulling the strings anymore."

Volunteers' narratives suggest that a variety of aspects of the year catalyzed introspection and self-understanding. First, for many volunteers being challenged in new ways was centrally important. Brenda, for instance, recalled: "It was in the rough times that I learned about myself; I was so sure about myself before, but the challenge in my year challenged me in how I live. It opened my eyes to who I was. It makes you see all your strengths and weaknesses and things you don't want to see in yourself."

Volunteers frequently reported learning through challenges or even "suffering," often spurring them to reflect on their role in the world. Others found that the new challenges of the year helped them to see how they behaved, reacted, and their own "limits" in new and different situations. Volunteers described feeling that after their year they, as one said, "know what [they] like and do not like" and how they operate in different environments. For instance, a woman who was India for her year reported her developing "sense of who I am" from her experiences, especially from being pushed outside her "comfort zone": "I've gained a sense of who I am. When I was out of my comfort zone I was more easily able to get to know myself and what I can handle and what I can't."

In addition, many volunteers felt that getting away from the pressures and culture of home (and off the "academic treadmill") was critical to facilitate introspection and self-understanding. As Kyle, a volunteer in Guyana, said, "You're free there—you can be yourself, which helps you understand yourself." In the case of Brenda, her gap year pushed her to discover more about herself as she was "challenged" in a space removed from her previous social life and family in Holland:

> I also looked at myself more because you have time to. You have time to think during your year . . . and you have no friends or family to keep you in one direction . . . the best thing about the gap year is that you have time to think without pressures from your life before. And during the gap year you can't fall back on family and friends—and you realize that, shit, I am a complete mess.

Other volunteers echoed this idea that space and distance from their previous lives facilitated their intrapersonal understanding. Leah, for example, said that being away from family and her "crowded life of work, friends and busyness gave [her] space to develop emotionally and [she] learned [her] strengths and weaknesses." Many other volunteers thought having free time was valuable for them in creating opportunities and a context for reflection. Brenda said: "Since we had nothing to do on the weekend . . . we had lots of time to think about ourselves and issues in the world."

In a similar vein, as a result of this reduced cultural and social pressure from their previous lives, some volunteers reported being more able to explore their identity by doing things that they could not do before their year. One recalled feeling that he could "experiment" and do things he would not otherwise have done at home, like "shaving [his] head." Another said that he had tried to join the army before his gap year but his mother wouldn't let him. He joined the army in Thailand on a one-year contract during his year (in addition to his volunteer teaching position) in "exchange for teaching English to the officers."

Being New

Volunteers, especially those in a rural setting, also felt that being a new entrant into a community—and the demands of building new relationships and the attention their arrival brought—instigated self-reflection and self-understanding. Leah illustrated how having to form new relationships with a new—and diverse—community encouraged introspection: "Before I was only friends with those from school, and I have known them for years . . . because you have to form new relationships there, you think about how you form them and why you do the things you do." Leah added that she can now "see the power of relationships" and how they can influence us, recalling: "I didn't think about that before because I didn't have to make new relationships—gap years force us into new relationships with lots of different people . . . you think about the first impression that you give off . . . to older and people my age." Another volunteer said this process helped her see "how I act and interact with others," and another said that it helped her to become "conscious of how I presented myself and its effect on others."

Volunteers often recounted the initial discomfort of being a newcomer into a community and someone who is different looking and the resulting greater "awareness" of self. Even though many volunteers wanted to integrate to the extent that they were considered a local, they often felt different from the local population and culture. One white volunteer in Honduras expressed his frustration that, in spite of his efforts to integrate and speak Spanish, there was a constant reminder that he was not one of them: "I wanted to look darker, but no matter how tan I was, I could never look like them." At the same time, however, volunteers often felt that their role in the community gave them a place and a home that helped to ground their growing comfort with themselves.

Some volunteers felt that channeling their focus off themselves and toward others, especially while building relationships with others, was an important catalyst to greater self-understanding during the year. As one participant said, "During the year you learn about yourself when you turn the focus off yourself—you talk to others and make friends—and you learn about others so you see differences." Another volunteer shared a similar observation: "We were interesting to the locals—they found us fascinating—they ask you questions—just as we were also fascinated with them. As you find out more, you reflect on yourself and why we are the way we are."

The long-term nature of the gap year allows for numerous new experiences (e.g., challenges with living with their volunteer partner, new interactions and relationships) that help the students to "understand themselves" in many lights. However, it was often not until volunteers returned that they came to see how they had changed from their year. Many said that coming back and noticing differences between themselves and their friends helped them to further understand their own formation and changes. For instance, one said: "I came back and my friends at home . . . they were all the same and hadn't changed. In my year, I was in a new community and changing, and that made me see how my home and community had formed me."

This process continued when volunteers entered college, as gap year participants differentiated themselves from others in their attitudes and understandings; one said: "Now that I am in university, I feel that I am more mature than many of the first year students because of my year." Gap year volunteers also differentiated themselves from other college students who took a gap year. A hierarchy of experiences, based on both location and length of time, exists among the gap year volunteers—with students who spent a year in the developing world near the top.

Independence

Volunteers commonly reported that their gap year experiences helped them become more independent. For many volunteers, it was the first time away from their parents for any extended period—and the first time living with what many described as "autonomy." Citing this, gap year participants came away with a feeling that they can "look after themselves" and are more independent. Holly highlighted this, attributing her new "independence" after her year to "living without parents" and being forced "to do things for [herself] and to combat difficult situations on [her] own."

In addition to living outside the support network of home, volunteers often described how the different and unique challenges of the year contributed to growth in independence. Janet highlighted this, citing the importance of being pushed outside one's "comfort zone": "I feel I've also started to know my boundaries and how far I can be stretched out of my comfort zone. It's a great feeling to know you can be much more independent than even you think you can be."

Volunteers also cited that having opportunities to exercise responsibility and face challenges was important in building this sense of independence. Bridget, a volunteer in China, reflected: "There were lots of challenges in China, but from these challenges I developed more self-reliance and more self-motivation." Another woman expressed how she developed greater independence from the "freedom of running my own life and being responsible for so much more than I ever had in the past." Tom, who volunteered in South Africa, echoed this relationship, explaining the independence he gained from the responsibility and autonomy he had in his volunteering role: "I think that our project threw us in the deep end. There was little help from our colleagues . . . However, it was a really good experience not to be helped and have to work it out for ourselves and to have the level of responsibility that we were given."

The growth in independence and autonomy was assisted by feeling more competent in practical matters of daily life. After his year in Uganda, David felt a "lot more mature and can honestly look after [himself], in terms of working and also in terms of domestic things such as cooking, cleaning, budgeting, etc." As illustrated above, the idea of feeling more independent is associated with confidence and "doing independence." That is, a feeling of independence grew as volunteers learned and completed tasks like cooking and cleaning but also with achievement in tasks done with greater autonomy (e.g., travel, volunteer work).

Control

In a related concept, volunteers' narratives suggested a change in the way they attributed the control they had over their own future and how they experienced the world. For instance, Kara, a former volunteer in Chile, said: "I also learned that you make your day as entertaining as you make it yourself." Jessica, a Dutch volunteer in India, thought that her most valuable lesson reflected this theme of control and her ability to determine how she makes meaning and interacts with the world: "I realized that you cannot always change the situation you're in, or how the people are around you, but only how you act on it and what you do with it. Even though sometimes the mistakes seem to be totally not on your side, I can only change what I do with it and how I act upon it."

The long-term nature of the experience also seemed to promote this development, because volunteers felt they could not "hide" all year. They were in their gap year community for a year, so they had to go out and engage with the community and environment around them. Laure, a volunteer in Cambodia, recalled her experience:

> When I arrived I was miserable . . . I stayed inside and cried a lot, but after a couple months I realized that if I don't do something then I am just going to sit here and be miserable . . . so I went out to the community and engaged more and eventually it was much better. From then on I realized that I was going to have to go out and make my year.

Similarly, volunteers' narratives suggest that the gap year often cultivated a feeling of personal responsibility. In fact, Jane, who volunteered in Uganda, claimed that the "year forces personal responsibility." Volunteers often believed that completing a gap year itself was a personal accomplishment; something aided by the fact that they had to fundraise for the year, often entertain themselves and create plans, and "make it" on their own often with little support during the year. One volunteer remarked that the gap year placement organization "allowed it to be my year, and I really appreciated that."

It seems that volunteers' professional roles in the community also influenced their growth in feeling more in control and a need to be responsible in their lives. This occurred as volunteers developed specific skills, such as becoming better organized or learning how to manage workloads, and became more proficient in their professional roles and living overseas. One remarked:

> I also think having a "proper" teaching role has made me more responsible and aware of the consequences of my actions. If I was late for school in Scotland the consequences weren't particularly great. However, punctuality and appearance at Junten are very important, as they are in most workplaces. I grew up a lot in this respect, perhaps more so than my friends who have part time jobs back in the UK.

Resilience and Emotional Regulation

In addition to feeling more capable and more autonomous, volunteers described feeling more resilient. Volunteers felt "less vulnerable," "tenacious," and "perseverant" after their year. Exemplifying this, Holly, a volunteer in Cambodia, "built up a level of resilience against circumstances that prior to my year would have majorly fazed me."

Volunteers recalled experiencing a range of intense emotions; one volunteer who worked in an orphanage in Uganda shared: "I cried a lot over my year . . . and I experienced a range of emotions." Experiencing these emotions—and getting through the year—seemed to contribute to this feeling of resilience. Ginger, a volunteer in China, highlighted this: "I had emotions that were so high and so low over my year—my emotional strength was tested; it was draining. But eventually you don't get so emotional because you get used to everything and you develop an emotional strength after being tested so much."

As a result of having gotten through these emotionally challenging circumstances, volunteers sometimes felt more in "control of their emotions" or emotionally "matured." Amanda, for example, said: "I am less hot headed, not so aggressive when I hear things. I am more matured." Another remarked, "I am more mature; I can react to things without escalating things. I have greater control and use reason more." Likewise, some described feeling more "patient," often after dealing with a year of many things, like bus schedules or expectations, not working out as they were accustomed. Jonathon, a volunteer who was in Uganda for the year, reflected: "I used to get bothered by things, like if the bus didn't show up on time, but now I am the complete opposite as I was before . . . I just say it will come when it comes." In another example, one volunteer in Japan stated he became more "patient" and "rational"—saying he "realized that it is not the end of the world if things don't work out the way you want them."

Contributing to this feeling of reduced emotional "escalation," volunteers described that because they developed broader worldviews and can see "larger" or "more important issues in the world" like poverty (which will be discussed further in chapters 4 and 5), they are less affected by what they saw as the "small things" in life.

Making a Difference

Building on the changes outlined above, volunteers frequently experienced a growth in their perception that they can make a difference in the world. Granted, making the decision to take a gap year already suggests that many volunteers have relatively higher levels of personal efficacy than many of their peers. However, their narratives show that the year further developed these feelings. Volunteers explained that because the gap year provides an opportunity to act in a context where there were consequences—and consequences that often had real effects on others—it helped to cultivate greater feelings of personal efficacy. Specifically, having "high" levels of responsibility where their performance affected others seemed to encourage volunteers to work hard, further building their own skill set and feelings of competence as they do so. Lindsay's narrative illustrated this:

> I really enjoyed the responsibility, having only been responsible for myself in the past. It was a really rewarding experience to know that if I worked hard and was enthusiastic these people in front of me would work harder and get better grades. . . . It felt and showed me I was doing the right thing. I guess I just liked to know what and how far I could be stretched; it felt good to be moved away from my comfort zone and to see what I was capable of achieving.

Likewise, a volunteer in India highlighted the role responsibility played for her: "I gained the most from situations where I was given a lot of responsibility— you don't know you can do it until you do it. I know now that I am more capable to do more things, like control a class, or really relate to people, I am confident in my own abilities."

Another element of the gap year that influenced volunteers' feeling of efficacy was volunteers' creation of "secondary projects" in the latter part of their gap year. These consisted of community-based projects designed to alleviate some social problem they had come to understand during their year (e.g., starting a tutoring or after-school sports program or a neighborhood garden). These secondary projects helped volunteers cultivate greater degrees of self-efficacy, and they are often proud that they know they can "make a difference" in the life of another.

This higher self-efficacy did not develop overnight. Early in their gap year, many volunteers often experienced frustration with their inability to perform their job, integrate, or feel like they are making a meaningful difference to the community. Reflecting his expectations before they year, one said: "The staff told us we were not going to 'change the world' out there, but you don't really believe them." Struggling with a limited impact during the year, one volunteer recalled questioning, "What am I doing here?" Often, volunteers' narratives suggest this led to a more limited, pragmatic, and realistic perspective of their potential impact, one often informed by the complexities of social and political change.

With a recalibration of expectations, many volunteers reported leaving the year feeling that they were able to make some difference to the lives of those in their care. Reflecting this, a volunteer in Uganda recalled: "I was an idealist when I went out, but I realized that I wasn't making the change that I thought I would. By the end, I had realized that I had probably made a difference in the lives of one or two children, but that was enough." Another shared: "I realized that I was not going to save the country. You are just one person from another country, and that's how they view you. The best you can do and hope for is to go in and become friends with them and learn about their culture, and you should be happy with that." Another volunteer, Nichole, expressed this after her year in Peru:

> Before my year, I never wanted to be naive enough to think that I could "make a difference." But that outlook has totally changed as a result of my year in Peru. Although I know I didn't change the world, I was lucky enough to be given the chance to see that the work I did actually really did make a direct difference to the children that I was working with.

As a result, volunteers typically reported feeling they were helped more than they were able to help others. Paulina, a volunteer in Peru, summed up her limited impact of her year and her new orientation: "The gap year is not about changing people's lives . . . it's about realizing that you want to change other people's lives."

These increased feelings of competence helped volunteers to see how they could contribute to the world (a topic discussed further in chapter 5). Heather, for example, illustrated her newfound understanding of herself and her ability to contribute: "Before my year, I thought: Why would anyone want help from me? What do I have to offer? Now I realize a lot. I can be a companion; I can be role model to kids; I can make a difference in the lives of others." After being a teacher during her year, one volunteer said she realized: "I have something special, something valuable to offer."

Higher self-efficacy has consequences when volunteers return to their home countries, and many report that they are more involved in their university and civil society after their gap year. Matt, a volunteer in Guyana, highlighted his growing desire to contribute: "Before my year I used to think about what I can get from society, but now I think about what I can give to society." John, a Ugandan volunteer, recalled a demonstration of his newfound sense of self: "After coming back from my year, I was walking on the street and saw a group of boys bullying another boy. I went over there and got the group to stop doing it, and that is something that I would have never done before my year."

Self-confidence

Volunteers experienced a near-universal sentiment of a growth in self-confidence. Allison explained that during her first lesson as a teacher in China: "I was shaking in front of the class, but now I can go and talk to anyone—I have much more confidence now." Some volunteers expressed a change in their understanding of confidence: Jason, for example, reported: "I realized that confidence is just a frame of mind; I feel like I can do anything now," and Susan, a volunteer in Honduras, said: "Before I thought self-confidence was about physical appearance . . . your looks . . . now I understand that it is much more than that—you have to have a belief in yourself and your values."

It seems that volunteers' perception that the gap year is a major challenge and obstacle—a challenge they felt they conquered themselves—helped them develop this confidence. Below, Jenna, a volunteer in the Dominican Republic, illustrates how her ideas about how she wanted to "do everything" during the year pushed her to try and experience more:

> I only have really been able to observe this recently on my return due to finding myself in familiar situations and reacting in a different way, but I have developed confidence in myself and my opinion. When I first went overseas I thought I was invincible and wanted to do everything, and so I seemed to put myself in these crazy situations topped with an unfamiliar language. I have found that very little back here pushes me to that point of panic like it used to. However, in general I feel there is very little of me that hasn't been affected or changed by my experiences overseas.

Often, volunteers were put in situations that encouraged them to engage in new and challenging experiences. For example, John, a volunteer in China, remarked, "I had to sing a song in front of the school . . . before at home I would rather have amputated my arm off, but I did it!" Similarly, when asked why he felt more confident after his year, Kyle, a volunteer in Guyana, said: "You were given massive responsibility, put in new situations, and pushed out of your comfort zones to realize that you can be in new situations and a new environment and do well." Further highlighting the importance of overcoming challenges in building self-confidence, Rosie, a volunteer in India, said:

> I felt challenged often this year, and now that I've come home, I can see how much I can actually do that I wouldn't have thought I could before. I got through

those challenges. That helps me to realize that I can get through anything if I try. I feel less panicky in daunting situations and able to deal with obstacles that I overcome because that is something I felt like I had to do a lot in India.

The professional nature of volunteers' placements seemed particularly important in this growth in confidence. Megan, a volunteer teacher in China, remarked:

I had shit self-confidence before. I was a teenager and unsure of myself. The gap year brings self-confidence on much more rapidly. I think it wouldn't have been until my late 20s or early 30s otherwise . . . It's also what people think of you, and after you stand up in front of 80 kids and teach and live in China for a year, you really feel that you can do anything.

As Megan suggests, teaching placements seemed to be particularly influential, especially as volunteers felt that they had to be confident and appear confident to their students to do their jobs well. Mark, a volunteer in Honduras, illustrated:

My greatest challenge was probably the teaching and the fact that I had to change very much as a person in order to have effective lessons with the children. Every day, no matter how I felt, I had to face up to these kids and teach them with confidence and energy, because that was the only way they were ever going to respond to me.

This increase in self-confidence seemed to contribute to volunteers' willingness and desire to take on new challenges and be more open to new experiences. Highlighting her increasing openness, Sara commented, "I am more open to new things, I have no fear in trying new things, and having them fail—I did that a lot in China." Indeed, many felt that that they were more interested and able to take on new challenges and opportunities or, as Lindsay said, "more willing to take on responsibility." In a similar vein, volunteers said they tried to "accomplish" more in their everyday lives after their year, as well as increased motivation when attempting a new task back in the United Kingdom. Ginger, for instance, described how she has reduced "inhibitions" now about taking on tasks; while Noel succinctly put it: "I try harder in things I do."

"Grown Up"

Building on the increased feelings of control, independence, and self-confidence, many volunteers described feeling more "grown up" or "adult," or generally more "mature" from their year. Ruth, a volunteer in Thailand, highlighted her new "adult" status after her year:

Since returning everyone has commented on how much more confident I am. I have always been confident with people my own age and younger but was always really nervous of "adults." Now I have turned into an adult myself and have become a lot more confident and not worried to speak up and have a joke with them.

These feelings of being more "adult" seemed to be influenced by their roles in their gap year community. Having more adult roles in the community over-seas—and being perceived as an adult while there—were especially helpful in contributing to this "grown up" feeling. Volunteers illustrated how working as an adult for the year contributed to their change in self-concept: "I grew up over my year . . . I had experience of living independently and working in a proper adult job." Another said: "I feel more mature, both in terms of being able to live independently and also feeling like I've actually lived and worked as an adult for a year, and been seen as one in a working environment."

Distinguishing oneself from others who are "less grown up" or "less mature" seemed to also be part of this feeling of adulthood, especially as volunteers took on roles as caretakers and teachers of younger children. As one said, "Going from being a student to a teacher just a couple months later" made him "grow up." Jesse, a volunteer in Thailand, illustrated how this was a gradual process for him, one largely derived from the role he played in the community:

I definitely feel like more of an adult now, but I don't know if there was any specific moment where I began to think of myself as an "adult." Being in a role of responsibility within the community forces you to act more mature. I think that by being treated as an adult (working full-time, being responsible for your own house and your own well-being) it forces you to be more adult. It was a very quick transition when I started teaching, into thinking of myself as an adult, because my role in the community was that of an adult. I guess I wouldn't say there was a moment when I started thinking of myself as an adult, I just was an adult, and still am an adult.

Leah, a volunteer in Namibia, and others felt that their feelings of "adulthood" were role dependent:

I found I thought of myself differently when I was in my different roles. When teaching/supervising, I think I felt a lot more "adult"—although sometimes I would describe it more as "aged" (after a particularly long or trying day). But when we got together with the other volunteers, I often really enjoyed the opportunity to be a "youth" again and relax without the pressures of responsibility that I experienced at work. I suppose we live up to the roles we have to fill—even though I didn't always feel I was responsible or mature, I had to act as though I was, and in doing so I suppose I became so.

Julie, a volunteer in Thailand, echoed this reflection in her first year of college:

I feel more adult now as I was completely responsible for myself, in cooking, cleaning and holding down a full time job. Our students and colleagues depended on us, so naturally I think we matured more because of that. Now, attending university, I can see that I am already a lot more independent, mature and confident in myself than others.

Being in the role of a caretaker seemed to encourage this change to a more "grown up" self-concept. Feeling responsibility for those in their care also had an effect, as Matt, a volunteer in Guyana, illustrated: "I had a lack of confidence in myself before my year . . . I was just a 17-year-old without responsibility. But teaching older boys and girls made me grow up. I had to be a role model for them." This was a similar sentiment that Leah expressed: "I was a role model for the young girls . . . I wanted to help guide them, and that made me conscious of how I acted."

In addition to contributing to feelings of being an adult, volunteers' narratives suggest that being perceived as a role model had positive consequences for personal development. Abigail, a volunteer in Malawi, used her feeling of being a role model for the children to monitor her own behavior: "I feel I was a good role model for the children at Yamikani. I rarely got angry and always made sure I listened to all sides of an argument. Because of this I found the children would come to me to ask my advice on disagreements or problems at school." Likewise, volunteers sometimes felt that they found role models themselves in the local communities that helped them. For instance, one volunteer in Botswana said of his boss, who was an former peace corps member and who had set up a school for orphaned boys: "Our boss was a really good man; a good role model for us . . . and we tried to keep up to his standard." On the other end, some volunteers reported that they did not like their bosses or hosts' behavior; some said they were "corrupt" or "unfriendly" people—and volunteers said they distinguished themselves from that behavior and tried especially hard *not* to be like them.

The perceived level of challenge of the volunteer's gap year and living situation influenced how adult some volunteers felt. Tobias, who spent his year in

Santiago, Chile, a city with which he was "disappointed that it was so similar to London" provided evidence of this relationship:

> Because I was still being cooked for and looked after by a family, I probably didn't experience as much of a change as other people. However, working as a teacher definitely made me feel a change. Spending the year having to act in front of the kids like my teachers at school had, made me see myself more as an adult. One boy thought I was in my twenties and the kids were surprised when my mum came over, because I think they saw me as just another teacher. Being perceived as an adult like that made the biggest difference. If I'd spent the year being treated by people at school as just a teenager who'd come over to help a bit, it wouldn't have been so effective. But the teachers and headmistress stressed to the pupils that we were members of staff.

Tobias's feeling that he did not experience as much change as other volunteers is quite an interesting one as we look into the pedagogy of the gap year and the issue of finding the optimal challenge for each volunteer. This element of the gap year will be discussed further in chapter 8.

Despite the limitations that Tobias felt, he described feeling more adult afterward, differentiating himself from his first-year peers in college, whom he saw as less adult. However, having adults treat him as a "young student," made it harder to maintain that status of adulthood, further illustrating how adulthood was somewhat context and perception dependent for the volunteers:

> Now at university, I do see myself as more adult, especially when I compare myself to some of the other first-years I've met at university. Some are 17 and leaving home for the first time so it's inevitable I think. However, having come back I'm treated by a lot of adults as a young student again, so it makes it harder to not see myself as one.

Body Image

Particularly for female volunteers, the gap year seemed to instigate changes in the ways some felt about their body image, and many reported a greater comfort with it after their year. A volunteer in Swaziland described her transition: "It was liberating there—without the same social pressures as the UK there—here there is so much pressure on everyone to look pretty, to wear heels, to go out and put on make-up every day to look pretty, but I didn't wear any for a year, and now I don't—it feels stupid." Likewise, a volunteer who spent her year in Thailand shared: "I used to cover up every little spot on my face with makeup but I don't care now; I don't wear any make up." Assimilating to the local way of life, another volunteer explained that since "you don't wear make-up overseas you get used to it and comfortable going out and not wearing it."

Holly, a final year college student who volunteered in India on her gap year four years prior to our interview, shared with me that her year "really changed" her. When she left for her year abroad, she brought a "hair straighter, make-up, and fake nails" and was worried about not being able to "dye her hair blond" again overseas. During her year, she recalled how she stopped using them and thought it was "ridiculous" that she had "brought all that stuff." Four years after her gap year, she continues not wearing make-up daily or dyeing her hair. Also growing in comfort with her image, one participant shared this: "*I* like what I look like and realized that that is what matters, even if no one else likes it." Another said: "I came back and my friend was complaining about how fat she was, and I was like, why are you doing that?"

As seen in volunteer reports of increased confidence, the professional roles of volunteers seemed to help change the way some felt about their appearance as they grew in confidence. Beth, a volunteer in South Africa, highlighted this dynamic: "I became more comfortable with my appearance over my year; as I grew in confidence it came with it. And you have to be confident and comfortable in situations there—especially when teaching so that the kids are too."

Mental Health Disorders

This subject provided possibly the most surprising responses from the volunteers and others I interviewed. As seen in the previous chapter on student motivations, quite a few people had mental health issues (e.g., anorexia, depression, etc.) and thought that going on a gap year would help resolve those issues. They sought to use the gap year as a way to "fix," to "cure" themselves, or to "run away." Before her year, one volunteer with bulimia remarked that her gap year "is the only light I can see out of this tunnel." Gap year provider staff members all felt that there has been an increase in volunteers dealing with these issues in recent years. Aware of the risks, provider organizations have knowingly accepted a few volunteers with a history of these illnesses, because they believe a gap year has the potential to be very positive for those who participate in it.

To be sure, there are substantial risks that are associated with sending these gap year volunteers abroad; the year is especially stressful and can lack support networks. Further, volunteers can feel they do not have control over what is happening around them, which can contribute to a relapse with an eating disorder or other mental health conditions. Given these risks, there is a mixed history with these types of cases. Sometimes, the gap year is seen by the volunteer as an "important part of the healing process," but other times during the year the mental health disorder reemerges. As one long-serving provider staff member put it, "These disorders have a bad habit of coming back during their gap year."

These mental health issues are complex, so I chose to include four stories of individuals who discussed with me at length their reflections on their gap year and their mental health issues. These examples begin a discussion on how these gap years might be of some help to volunteers with a history of mental health disorders. Removal from their home environment, serving others, support networks, seeing the world from a different perspective, feeling as a role model, religion, reflection, and a sense of accomplishment all seem to be elements of the gap year experience that volunteers felt might be part of a "healing process." This may not always be the case, however—gap years seem, in fact, to occasionally help retrigger a disorder. There are risks associated with sending these often more "vulnerable" volunteers overseas, to places with little mental health support and into situations where they are likely to experience trauma or harmful pressures. The experiences of these four suggest that serious reflection is warranted on whom to send, what project to send them to, and how to support volunteers overseas and when they return. This issue will be discussed further in chapter 8.

Leah

Leah was a volunteer in Namibia in 2009 who felt she had a very successful gap year. Leah was dealing with anorexia before and during her year, but by the time she departed the provider's debriefing session after her time overseas, she remarked to the staff, "You set me free; thank you." In the case below, I try to outline what about the gap year experiences helped her to feel that way.

Leah described her gap year as an "important part of the healing process" and that "before the year, [she] felt [she] wasn't in control of things." She said she did not "set out and think that this was going to fix me—but getting ready for my gap year gave me something to focus on and think about other than food." Struggling with her weight before the provider's selection course, her parents told her, "If you go up looking like that—they won't select you," so Leah said she "worked on gaining weight." After selection, Leah recalled that the organization said that they "wanted to send her," but that she "needed to gain weight to be healthy" before they would. As a result, Leah said that she motivated herself and "before training I gained some weight—working towards something took my mind off the focus on food."

In Namibia, Leah described the environment as "liberating for her" and that there was "less pressure there; there were not magazines there like in the UK" that pressured her to look a certain way. Importantly, Leah said that the year "helped to change my orientation to food—my perspective on food." She explained:

> Namibia had different ideas about food—different conceptions—food is part
> of culture there more, part of socializing more, and I wanted to take part in the
> culture, to not be rude, plus it was really tasty . . . I lived in the school hostel
> where meals were prepared for us, and also that people made food as a gift to me
> . . . The younger kids there couldn't understand anorexia; they couldn't under-
> stand why you wouldn't want to eat food.

There were other experiences that Leah reported as important parts of her year that helped to sustain a new perspective and her healthier lifestyle. Leah described her year as an "emotional year" in which she dealt with "personal issues." She said that before her gap year she was a "depressed, lonely, 17-year-old" who was also an atheist, having been a Christian before and raised in a Christian family. However, she recalled how religion helped her over the year:

> Over time in my gap year I became a passionate Christian. When I went out
> there, I didn't know people to rely on; I was stripped of social support—God was
> the only foundation. I had no one out there to see me through, so I had to rely
> on faith. And God spoke to me in new and exciting ways over my year. I worked
> in a Christian school, and there was a strong Christian community fellowship. I
> made friends with older people who were more spiritually mature—I got bogged
> down in teenage issues and they brought me up and offered new insight.

During her time in Namibia, she saw a Christian spiritual counselor and became active in the church community. She recalled: "It was an ongoing process that developed over the year . . . in the past, I sought approval from guys—instead of God . . . and over my year I realized how relationships have defined me and damaged me in many respects."

Leah said she is now "passionate about living in a Christian community; it helped me in times of need, and I want to be part of it." Leah also had her parents for support over the year. She wrote to them, reflecting and sharing personal issues with her parents, building her relationship with them over the year.

Together, Leah developed support in her project placement, and this support network seemed especially helpful for her.

At the same time, Leah believed that being removed from the United Kingdom gave her "space to develop emotionally." She explained:

> I was always busy in my crowded life before, with work, friends. I was just busy. That was taken away, so I had space to think about myself, and there literally is a lot of big open space in Namibia for personal reflection. The year helped me to learn about myself, learn my strengths and weaknesses, what I enjoy doing and dislike, and what I'm good at. I also learned what triggers certain emotions— after conversations I would reflect on why it affected me in a certain way—why I react in that way. I learned the importance of asking questions and reflection—I learned a lot of value in seeking reflection.

In addition, her role as a teacher helped her to develop her "self-confidence, strength, and patience." She said she gained a "confidence talking to others. I wanted to cry in front of my class, but that was not professional; I learned to keep my cool, use different teaching techniques to be calm in times of stress and conflict." Leah even began a group for Christian girls during her year. She remarked, "I was a role model for the young girls; I wanted to help guide them, and that made me conscious of how I acted." In fact, Leah believed that "reaching out to young girls, mentoring" is what she now wants to do in a career.

Finally, Leah described how the poverty in Namibia was also a challenge for her:

> I had not faced poverty before; seeing it created new emotions. The poverty and suffering was a challenge for me and my faith, but I saw how God blessed us when we were working for others. The challenge pushed me to be more about how to serve others, and I learned to place others' priorities higher than my own priorities. I challenged myself to use my free time for others, and I saw that serving others doesn't have to be a burden.

Serving and working for others in her role during her gap year seemed to help Leah develop an "others-focused" orientation, an orientation that seemed important in Leah's "healing process."

Jesse

Jesse was a volunteer in Thailand who dealt with depression over his year and believed his year teaching, like Leah's, was an important part of his healing process. He said it helped him to "reconstitute" himself. He recalled: "I was depressed before; I changed schools and I had no friends . . . the gap year was important for me; I just really needed something to change in my life, and the gap year was a way to change everything." Jesse remarked that "a lot of healing happened before I left . . . as I focused on the year. But the year showed me what life could be like, what I could have." He explained how the year served as a space for him to explore identity:

> During the gap year you can define yourself because you have no specific reputation there; it is your year. I feel like in school you have defined roles that you continue from before; you are always comparing yourself to the year above and year below you, to fill a role. You live in the shadow of the year above you. Away on your year, you are in a new place, away from that society.

Jesse reflected that the year "helped me to grow into myself; to see life from a very different perspective was really helpful for me." However, he said: "I was worried that I would get too comfortable in Thailand and think that all those issues [back home] don't matter—and not deal with them." In elaborating on how he dealt with them, he recalled:

> I don't know, just seeing life from another perspective, gaining confidence, and I was also just busy there—the first day we arrived we started teaching. There wasn't a lot of time to just focus on myself and issues; you had to focus on others. Serving others so much helped with the depression; you find what you care about and you focus on them.

Similarly, Jesse added that "During the year you learn about yourself when you turn the focus off yourself—you talk to others and make friends—and you learn about others so you see differences." Finally, Jesse felt that completing his gap year was an accomplishment, something he felt was important in his healing process: "The year was such an accomplishment, a self-achievement, a personalized achievement. You raise your own money to go out; you make it your own year."

Jennie

The final two stories are not as successful as Jesse's and Leah's. Jennie spent her year in the Dominican Republic, and I interviewed her shortly after she returned. She revealed that she struggled with food over her year. In fact, she said that even though she didn't have a "healthy relationship with food" before her year, she felt she "developed an eating disorder overseas."

Whereas Leah felt that Namibia was a liberating environment, Jennie felt very differently about her environment in the Dominican Republic:

> In the Dom Rep people commented on my body every day; it made me more self-conscious. In the Dominican Republic people tell you that you look fat, or they comment about your body, like "you have no ass." It was very sexualized and they really cared about image.... The father of one of my students hit on me too; I was trying to meet with him about his son in my class, and he said if my child can't pay attention to someone with a body like that than something is wrong with him. And I was not free from Western life in the D.R. It was driving me mental; it was so American. They want the same thing as the West, just different ways of going about getting them.

Jennie further explained her relationship with food: "I didn't have a healthy relationship with food overseas. It was a control thing; I could control my body and the ways boys saw me and how attracted they were to me. It was a pressurized organization too, and I rebelled with food. Actually, the director of the organization there said the volunteer last year developed an eating disorder too." In addition, Jennie reported that, "I felt out of my depth, and I wanted someone to take care of me, a man, a boyfriend."

Unlike Leah, who said her parents made efforts to support her, Jennie explained that she only talked to her father once over the year on his birthday and that "my relationship with my father became worse because of my year; it was bad before but he now still wants to try and treat me like a young kid and control my life . . . so I left for a week and lived with friends when I came back."

Coming back from her gap year, Jennie remarked, "People said I was tan and skinny; now I have to keep up that reputation; I hate that they didn't care about what I did over my year, only about my looks." She added that: "I am now more selective about the people I want to be around and be near me." After her year, Jennie went on to study philosophy and politics at college with a new interest in international affairs. Although she felt she gained a great deal from her year and had accomplished something, she also said, "I don't think I achieved my potential."

Katherine

Katherine, a volunteer who worked with disabled children in a school in South Africa for a year, is a slightly different case, included here to illustrate some of the emotional trauma volunteers sometimes faced working overseas. Katherine struggled with the emotional trauma she felt from her gap year even a year into college. Over her year, Katherine felt that she developed very deep connections to the children in her care. However, one event was particularly challenging for her. Months into her year, she discovered that one of the children at her school with Down syndrome had been raped. Katherine said that it was "really, really hard, so difficult to deal with because they become like your own children . . . and plus we weren't allowed to talk about it."

At her interview with me a year after returning from her gap year, Katherine remarked:

> I feel like I can't cry anymore, like I cried all my tears out over my year. I used to be a big crier, normally if I had just talked about that I would have been crying my eyes out, but I have developed a wall. I can't really cry about things. I think because I've blocked it all out; it was really hard for me to leave the girls, and I just developed a wall. I need to show emotion for my drama performances, and I used to be able to cry on command, but now I can't. I do feel sometimes that I need to cry and let anger out, but I just can't.

Katherine believed that she would have benefited if she had been offered some further counseling after her gap year.

Analysis

In this chapter, I focused on volunteers' reported changes in intrapersonal dimensions; in other words, how they understand themselves. Many of these intrapersonal changes seem to be associated with their discovering more qualities about themselves and seeing differences through developing new relationships and engaging in situations that were challenging. According to the narratives, the adversity and problems that these gap years presented to volunteers—who largely had to resolve them independently—seemed to help magnify these changes in self-perception. As one volunteer said: "I've realized that you don't know yourself until you put yourself into an unfamiliar situation. . . . I've found I'm much more capable than I dreamed of." This seems understandable; the gap year was the first time that most of the volunteers had lived away from their families, much less taken on a professional role in a foreign country. This finding also supports Bandura's (1986) hypothesis that self-confidence increases when a person successfully meets a number of challenges.

Illustrated in the case of Brenda, a volunteer in rural Honduras, the challenge of gap year experiences facilitated introspection and self-clarification. Volunteers reported that they developed a greater understanding and comfort with themselves, are not as susceptible to "what other people think," and thus feel they have more control over their lives. Brenda, who described her year as "really challenging," said that the year "forced" her to look at herself, to see herself for the first time. In Brenda's case, this led to a way of thinking about herself in which she can be who she wants to be and that no one "is pulling the strings anymore." In this, Brenda highlights a movement toward a greater ability to direct her own life, to trust her own internal voice, or a growing capacity for self-authorship.

Many volunteers also described how they felt they were more "adult" after their year, especially as they had "adult" roles in the community, operated more independently, and were perceived by others to be adults. This suggests that for these volunteers, adulthood was not seen as a fixed point in life but more a performance (King 2007); that is, the emergence of adulthood was linked to both occupying adult roles and being perceived as an adult by oneself and others.

The intensity of the dissonance and challenge was great in Brenda's case, which highlights the role of challenge in instigating reforms in the ways we understand the world. Our assumptions about the world can be deep seated and held with force and emotion (Mezirow 2000). Engaging and challenging them may be necessary to foster the critical reflection that self-authorship and transformational learning thinkers suggest. These findings support Teresa Donahue's (2009) research on study abroad where she suggested that programs that promoted transformative learning in students were the ones that challenged students the most.

Although the design of this study does permit robust comparison, the growth in self-understanding, self-efficacy, and confidence reported by volunteers here resonates with the findings from other experiential forms of learning (e.g., service-learning and study abroad). These findings also support Andrew King's (2007) hypothesis that a gap year can be a time and context for volunteers to do "identity work." However, we might predict that the magnitude or diversity of the reported impact will be greater here than in other experiential programs given the greater differences encountered, the intensity of the psychological engagement, longer duration, and often greater responsibility than most civic/volunteer programs in schools or higher education. As Janet Eyler and Dwight Giles (1999) suggest, placing volunteers in situations where they are likely to feel they have "real" and "authentic" opportunities to help others seems to be helpful to foster these changes. Participants reported an authenticity in their situations as members of their gap year communities with possibilities to help

others, a matter that will be discussed in greater length in the chapter on changing civic and religious perceptions.

The volunteers' experiences depicted in this chapter, which document the
relatively high degrees of independence afforded the volunteers and the resulting intrapersonal changes, are in contrast to Heath's (2007, 97) suggestion:

> Gap year organizations offering overseas volunteering opportunities provide a
> similarly protected experience, with students reliant on provider organizations
> for most if not all aspects of their trip. Overseas volunteering thus becomes a
> relatively risk-free, supervised and controlled experience. These developments
> are somewhat at odds with the assumption that overseas travel provides evidence
> of attributes such as independence and self-initiative.

This study details how these gap year volunteer placements, while structured,
typically offer a high degree of freedom, autonomy, and encourage travel in the
gap year country's region under little supervision—experiences that volunteers
reported contributed to the intrapersonal changes described in this chapter.

My study of gap years, unlike those in the literatures reviewed, identified a
number of volunteers who took a gap year with a desire to use the experience
to improve a mental health issue (e.g., depression, eating disorders). In this
chapter, I included a number of case studies to begin to examine the complex
interaction between the gap year experiences and volunteers with mental health
disorders.

There has been very little research to date on the role volunteering can play
in people's lives with respect to body image or mental health disorders (Howlett
2004). That said, there is some general research on volunteering that found
statistical evidence linking increased well-being and volunteering (Howlett 2004).
This relationship is not entirely understood, but some have suggested that participation itself, and feeling part of a social group or having a social role, may
lead to improved mental health (Wilson and Musick 1999). In addition, previous research suggests that volunteering can improve mental health by giving
participants greater purpose, confidence, and self-esteem (Wilson and Musick
1999). Recent research showed that helping others can help recovery and di-
minish egocentrism or selfishness among addicts (Pagano et al. 2010). As a general observation, Pagano et al. write, "When humans help others regardless of a
shared condition, they appear to live longer and happier lives" (2010, 31).

Building on this previous research, this study's findings begin a discussion
into the complex ways an international volunteering gap year might be, as one

volunteer said, an "important part of the healing process" for those with a history of mental illness. These gap years seem to have provided roles and experiences that gave greater purpose to some volunteers with mental illness, roles that included them in community life, and provided opportunities to work toward the well-being of others—experiences that the literature suggests may be helpful. Further, the gap year often led to improved confidence and provided an environment removed from many of the pressures of their previous lives in the West, an environment where new relationships can be built, pressures (especially for those with eating disorders) to have thin body types may be reduced, and different conceptions of food may be present. Coincidentally, the gap year, as a time where volunteers are often encouraged to explore a greater freedom in their lives and engage in new activities, overlaps with some new treatments for those with anorexia where patients engage in a variety of new activities (e.g., helping others and outdoor adventures) to "help patients become less rigid in their thinking" (Lambert 2010).

Because this study is not grounded in medicine or clinical psychology and employs a limited qualitative sample, no strong claims can be made about mental illness here. However, these findings do begin a discussion about how a gap year with a substantial change in environment, coupled with helping others, new activities, and being seen as a role model, might be helpful for some volunteers with a history of mental health disorders. However, it is very important to note that mental health illnesses can be—and were as some volunteers noted in this study—triggered by the stress and challenges of volunteering, especially overseas, where there are more challenges and can be weaker support networks and less access to treatment than previously in their lives. Volunteers also reported feeling a particular lack of control over their environment overseas, which contributed to Jennie, for example, trying to control her body more, manifesting in an eating disorder.

The discussion of volunteers' perceived changes in intrapersonal realms continues in chapter 6. There, I try to situate the volunteers' experiences in the lens of the pedagogical and social science theory. In the next chapter, I look at how the students changed in more interpersonal ways.

3

Changes in Relationships

The Importance of Relationships during the Gap Year

Relationships played an important part in the gap year; in fact, volunteers sometimes said that the relationships they made were the highlight of their year, the way they learned the most about the country, or even the principal cause of their changes from the gap year. These relationships were wide-ranging; volunteers developed close friendships and "intense relationships" with local people, their volunteering partner, and other gap year volunteers. Even more, volunteers often thought of their friendships with local people as a benchmark of their integration into the local community. Gap year participants felt that the long-term nature of the program was especially helpful in developing relationships with local people. One expressed that "local people are far more likely to invest in you if you're not just passing through and you are living there—those relationships, those friendships and bonds you create, they make the year so special."

Volunteers shared how they continued relationships with people from their gap year experiences through college—and some, for many years after college. It was common for them to return to their gap year community, often during summer breaks, and to keep in touch with friends abroad through letters, email, social media sites, research, or even financial support or advocacy.

Engaging with Others

With the volunteers' increased senses of agency, confidence, and self-understanding discussed in the previous chapter, participants often described changes in how they interacted with others after their year. Many found it easier to engage with others effectively. Florence attributed this to the confidence and self-knowledge she gained volunteering in South Africa: "Overall, I feel a greater confidence in myself, in my abilities to work with children and live and make friends with so many different people. I have also found that I know myself better in different situations and I am now more inclined to meeting new people without feeling shy and reserved." Maria felt a similar effect from volunteering in India: "I have a greater perspective of the world and that has helped me to be more confident around people who I don't know. I feel like I can talk easily with people I meet for the first time and I have a lot of confidence around kids."

Participants saw their year as improving their social skills, public speaking skills, or other social competencies. Robert, for instance, said: "I feel I have far more confidence talking to different kinds of people. The ability to speak my mind in large groups has improved." Likewise, Liz, a volunteer in Cambodia, emphasized her new interpersonal capabilities: "Possibly the most valuable skill I have gained whilst being overseas is confidence. I am now able to speak well and with an air of confidence to big groups and also can adapt to interacting with new people more efficiently than I could before I went away."

Volunteers also felt better able to interact with a broad range of people. Highlighting this, Becky shared the following: "My interpersonal and communication skills have improved from my experiences over the year, as I gained a lot of experience involving dealing with people, whether they are very young children, older children or adults." Like Becky, many felt that their life in their hometowns had primarily involved interacting with peers, while their gap year induced interactions with people of all ages and from different cultures. This was certainly true of Holly, a volunteer in Honduras: "Before, I lived in a bubble of friends and people my age. Now I genuinely enjoy being with people of all ages." Another volunteer said: "I'm more able to relate to more people because I met people I would not otherwise have met."

Volunteers also thought this breadth of social experience made them more open-minded about others. As one put it: "I get on with people better—over the gap year you meet new people; you become more open minded about others. I really try not to go on first impressions anymore . . . and plus I am more confident so I can engage with more people."

The resulting interpersonal confidence often made volunteers more willing to meet others and make new friends. For instance, one volunteer shared: "I am more interested in people now. I see they have more to offer, and so do I." A volunteer in Japan, who said he "didn't have a lot of friends in high school" and that he made some good friends over his year, reported that "going to university, I am now excited to make new friends." Tobias, a volunteer in Chile who wanted to use the year to become more "extroverted," said: "Talking to other people was a chore before . . . but I don't feel that way anymore. I am more confident with others, and I had some genuine, interesting conversations . . . I realized that we have much to learn from others." However, Tobias's case also suggests that not all gap year placements and experiences are equally powerful. He felt that in Santiago, a large city, he was not "forced" to develop relationships and that there was "pressure" to remain anonymous in the big city. This issue will be further discussed in chapter 8.

Volunteers cited the specific culture into which they were placed as a prime influence on how they changed in relationship to others. They highlighted the impact of being "shaped" or influenced by the local culture and environment. Kaitlin, a volunteer in Thailand, felt that she became so accustomed to sharing and helping her friends in Thailand that she is now much more "kind and generous . . . I was shaped by Thai people." Kaitlin also gave an example of how her behavior has changed: "Since being back in the UK, I have been doing more things to help friends, like sharing and giving lifts. Like the other day when I opened the pack of cookies; I put it on the table to give it to friends, but they were hesitant to take it, people wanted to pay me, but I didn't want that. I forgot that we do exchanges in England." Another volunteer, Matt, felt changed by his year in Guyana:

> One thing I know I gained is confidence and a completely new perspective on life in England. Everybody over in Guyana is extremely confident in themselves and don't put themselves down all the time and can very easily talk in front of a large group without getting nervous. I also learnt to do this in my own way. My confidence definitely increased during my time away. Now being home I don't hide away in large groups but start talking and joining in more conversations.

But extroversion was not the only effect. One volunteer stated that the generosity of the Thai people made him more "caring and empathetic . . . in Thailand there is nothing more important than giving your time and caring about others." A volunteer in China said that the "main thing I took away was kindness; always try and give to others . . . the people were so generous and kind . . . it rubbed off on me." Another volunteer said Japanese culture influenced him to pay others more respect: "I am more polite now; I respect elders and others now; I also say 'please' and 'thank you' more."

More than general confidence and empathy, gap year participants specifically reported improvements in their ability to communicate across cultural divides. A volunteer who went to Thailand explained that, although it was his "greatest challenge," he learned to "interact with people from a different culture." He added: "I didn't realize quite how ensconced in my English culture I was; I had to learn new ways of joking and talking so I could be understood." Tom, a volunteer in South Africa, remarked that after having to deal with new and culturally sensitive situations over the year, "I have learned when not to speak my mind and employ a lot more tact when speaking to people."

These forms of interpersonal growth were sometimes stimulated by volunteers' particular roles in their host communities. They were typically placed in helping professions that demand a high level of empathy, working with children and others in their care as teachers or social workers. One said he became more compassionate and empathetic after being a teacher, explaining: "I learned to see when the kids are having trouble, learning to help them." Volunteers also reported experiencing intense emotions over the year that helped them to be more empathetic. For instance, one volunteer who worked in an orphanage recalled: "I cried a lot, and I experienced a range of emotions; now I am more sensitive and aware of others' emotions."

Tolerance and Understanding of Others

Their time overseas made gap year participants more tolerant and better able to see things from another's perspective. Having to learn from and interact with others was often cited as the main cause of this change. John, who spent his time in Japan, reflected: "I think my general attitude to non-Brits has become much less pessimistic or cynical. Meeting so many different types of people here has made me much less judgmental of people before I meet them." Many felt more open to others and new experiences and reported an increased curiosity about new cultures and ways of being. Becky, a volunteer in Peru, said after her year: "I feel I am less judgmental and open-minded to accept all types of people and cultures. And I feel I want to understand all types of cultures in the world. I feel more mature, relaxed, and confident in myself." It seems that the improved self-confidence and self-understanding discussed previously helped volunteers to engage more tolerantly with others.

Another aftereffect of the gap year was that participants felt that they could more easily "relate to others" from different backgrounds, motivated by a growing recognition of their basic commonality. Helen, a volunteer in India, highlighted this:

> I found returning to Britain and listening to some people's opinions quite distressing as many voiced their prejudice and suspicion of Muslims and other ethnic minority groups. Living overseas I judged people individually on their actions not by their nationality, race or religion. I found that though our views differ, the qualities we admire in friends and colleagues are universal.

Similarly, Kara, who lived in Chile, said she "gained a respect for other people, being friendly and interested in other people no matter their ethnicity, race, color or beliefs."

Gap year participants also reported that their year, especially their volunteering position, contributed to a more "patient," "understanding," or generally positive perspective on others—suggesting a greater depth in their evaluations of others. Nancy, a volunteer in Peru, felt that her more patient and understanding disposition allowed her to "no longer judge people in the way I sometimes used to." John, who taught and worked in a home for troubled boys in Botswana, echoed this: "I really cared for the boys" and "dealing with the boys has given me more patience and a wider understanding of why some people are the way they are." Finally, David, who also worked with troubled boys in Botswana, explained his new position toward others:

> I have come to realize that there are no stupid people in the world. Everyone has their own abilities and it just takes time to find those skills. Whether a person is a genius at math or is excellent at chopping firewood, everyone has their own admirable qualities. Also, when at first you think some people are just rotten, if you try to get to know them a little you realize that they have a good side and this good side just needs to be encouraged and drawn out.

Partner Relationships

Volunteers' relationships with their partner—the other gap year volunteer or volunteers in the same project and living space—seemed to be particularly influential, especially in interpersonal dimensions.

Living with another person in a foreign country in close quarters for a year put participants under unique pressures. On occasion volunteers even had to share the same bed for a year. In any case, participants had essentially no choice but to live with their partner—there is a "permanence," as one volunteer described it, to this relationship. Volunteers found these relationships intense, often even likening them to marriages or sibling relationships. James and John, for instance, said: "It was like we were married. We spent even more time together than a married couple because we worked together." Another partnership expressed this intimacy after returning: "We are like brothers now—not mates." One partnership, where both volunteers attended the same university after they returned, said: "We became like brothers, even two years later we still meet up and talk and help each other—we are incredibly close."

In addition to the "permanence" and intimacy of these relationships, some of the volunteers highlighted another interesting aspect: their exclusivity. As one put it: "We were close . . . it creates a bond knowing that I was the only other person who understood what happened in the year." These partnerships were also often critical in a volunteer's support network during the year. For instance, one volunteer said that he and his partner "were each other's only source of home comfort." Another volunteer shared: "I formed an amazing friendship with my partner. We worked so well together and helped each other through hard times."

However, volunteers also often recalled having some turbulence in these relationships as they learned to live with each other. As one said:

> When we first met on training we did not like each other, and I thought we would have a terrible year—and we did have a falling out in the beginning because of work, stress, sharing a room—but eventually we figured out our arrangements— one organizes and plans more. We figured out each other—then our relationship became good.

Likewise, another shared: "We had to figure out the power dynamics of our relationship before it was better," while another happily admitted: "I did not think we would get on at first—but we did—we just talked about problems . . . and now I don't think I could have a better friend for life."

To be sure, not all volunteer partnerships developed the same "sibling-like" intimacy. Nevertheless, volunteers were typically able to establish at least a professional, working relationship to get through the year. Sam, a volunteer who was in an urban area in Japan, said that even though his partner and he were more like "acquaintances" than "brothers," he felt that "it worked out because we were both interested in different parts of Japan." Two partnered volunteers in an urban area of Capetown, South Africa, reported that they did not become like brothers "but more like friends." One member of the partnership said this:

> I had my own space so I could use it and if I needed to get away often—and I definitely needed to—I would go to the neighbor's flat. My partner was so lazy—I had to tell him when to get up—etc.—if I didn't plan anything, he would just sit inside and watch TV for hours.

These latter examples were often from volunteers in cities, suggesting that urban areas may do less to foster intimacy, because there are more spaces for partners to "get away" and more opportunities for socializing or entertainment outside the relationship.

Volunteers developed a variety of new skills from these partnerships, such as the ability to "compromise," or greater "patience in relationships." Janie, a volunteer in Peru, described how this happened for her: "The relationship I had with my partner needed a lot of patience. I think I was very lucky in the partner I got, but having a forced relationship had its rough patches and patience always helped a lot in that case too, which helped me become more patient in other relationships." Others said living closely with another helped them learn how to better share, as Dominic highlighted: "I feel like I have a greater ability to share now, including my personal space, and I'm less selfish after sharing a room and my belongings."

Volunteers often said that their relationships with their partners also helped them to become "more aware" of how their actions affected others. Tamara, a volunteer in Uganda, attributed this to the partnership's public unity: "Because you are inseparable from your partner, and seen as that way by others, you are like one person. You always think: How is this going to affect my partner and how is my partner going to deal with my actions?" Likewise, another volunteer recalled: "I think I became more aware of the effects of my actions on others . . . I also developed more of an idea of what people thought about me from my partner."

Many volunteers also believed that these partnerships taught them the importance of communication in relationships and methods for managing conflict. Vicky shared her experience with this: "I had a problem with my partner—she didn't know I didn't like what she was doing—I had to open up and tell her—we had to talk, and we learned the value of communication in relationships." However, people learned to be more strategic about their communication; that is, the need to sometimes, as volunteers put it, "pick their battles" and "let things go." For instance, when two partners returned home at the end of their year, one explained:

> We are very different—he is the loud outgoing one—and I am the shy quiet
> one—but instead of being in conflict, we complemented each other. I became
> more loud and outgoing. We became like sisters—so there is no point in bringing
> up things that bother you. You have to get on, unless it really bothers you. You
> put up with it—or ignore it.

Volunteers also believed that their partnership would help them in future living situations and in getting along with those who are different. One said that living with a partner will "make it a lot easier to live with another person who I don't know." In discussing her partner relationship, another volunteer recalled: "I have learnt how to get on with someone who I probably would never be friends with, had I not been put with her. We probably wouldn't have met, even if we were in the same room. I can now be very tolerant of people who are totally different from me in seemingly every way." In addition, Megan, a volunteer in China, reported that she learned "how to deal with people you don't like." In college, volunteers said they felt that they were more easily able to transition to shared university accommodation and "live and share space" with new people because of their year. Amy shared the impact of her partnership on her interpersonal development:

> I really learned how to treat people and the need for diplomacy . . . in university
> my friends gossip and talk and bitch at each other, but I think "aren't we a bit
> older than that now" . . . My partner helped with that because I was with her 24/7
> and after a while you just realize that you have to let things go with people.

The dynamics of these partner relationships were sometimes purposefully designed by the gap year provider to benefit a volunteer. Staff placed, for example, confident volunteers with shyer ones, in the hope that one would help the other gain confidence and integrate in the community. A volunteer from such a partnership explains how this occurred in her situation: "My partner was more confident and outgoing than me; she pushed me overseas to do more, to go local, to places and restaurants I did not want to. But I'm glad I did; now I am not afraid of so many new places." Similarly, Katherine, a South Africa volunteer, reflected on her dynamic with her partner:

When we first arrived, Becky was quite shy and reserved. When we went out I would always have to go introduce myself and say, "Hi, I am Katherine and this is Becky," but, as the year went on, she got more confident, and I kinda pushed her too. I would say "why don't you go introduce us," and toward the end of year she was much more confident and outgoing.

However, some extroverted volunteers shared that they felt they were being "used" to educate the other volunteer; one even said it was "somewhat annoying" to have been placed with a shy volunteer.

The fact that volunteer partnerships are limited by the provider to two or very rarely three people seems to have had a significant effect on the experience. These smaller units seemed to encourage volunteer integration in the local community and culture, an especially important element of any transforming gap year. As one volunteer said: "With only two of us, the people there were not as intimidated and more likely to approach us compared to large groups of foreigners. They are more likely to invite you out . . . with larger groups they can feel that you are already doing your own things with your group." In a similar vein, a volunteer in Guyana said: "My partner left during the year, but I developed really close friendships there with the people because I was there by myself." This matter will be addressed further in chapter 8 on designing the gap year.

Reflections on Strangers and Relationships

Volunteers often experienced changes in their general attitudes toward people that they do not know. Specifically, several volunteers reported that they trust others and strangers more than they did before their year. One person who spent his year in South Africa said: "Before my year, I would have been negatively disposed to people I didn't know, kind of expecting the worst. But I think that has flipped now, and I expect a positive response." Abigail's time in Malawi warmed her up to others: "I have more faith in people now; the people in Malawi are generally very friendly and honest, which is reassuring when every day in the UK you hear about the terrible things people do!" Another volunteer echoed this shift: "I put quite a bit more trust in strangers now, especially after hitchhiking in South Africa. You can trust people more than you expect." In fact, several volunteers said they now criticize their home country for what they called a "stranger-danger" mentality and the message to young people that they should generally fear unknown people.

Receiving help during times of need seemed especially influential in changing volunteers' conceptions of strangers. For instance, one said: "Before India I feared that no one would speak to me; no one would help me, but it wasn't like that—people were friendly and helpful." This shift in perception of strangers was more common among volunteers in rural areas. By contrast, a few people staying in larger cities reported becoming more fearful or cautious of strangers, especially if they were victims of a crime like robbery during the year. For instance, a young woman who was robbed by a group of black South African teenagers said that now when she now sees a group of black men on the street she is "fearful." Volunteers' changes in views of the "other" more generally will be discussed further in chapter 5.

Beyond volunteers' attitudes toward strangers in particular, they also became more concerned about others in general and placed a greater importance on relationships in their lives. Megan, a volunteer from China, highlighted this perceived shift: "I am much more humble from my year; I think of others much more, and I put others' interests before my own . . . I think I am more selfless now, but it's ironic because I feel selfish. I go to do selfless things for others—but I gain so much back—I can't win." Suggesting that volunteers' work in helping professions influenced this, one said: "We worked really hard over the year. It was really challenging; it was ingrained in us to help other people."

Volunteers often found relationships "more important" after their year. One said that she is "prioritizing her values" in her everyday life to make "relationships and others more important." Similarly, Mark, a volunteer in Guyana, said: "I think that I have definitely grown up more as a person and have discovered the important things in life like friends and family. Also I am now no longer too busy for people, if they need my help I will offer." People sometimes cited the local culture as an influence on their growing sense of the importance of relationships. For example, a volunteer in India remarked: "Relationships are more important for me . . . in India relationships are so important, just look at their weddings."

Their narratives also suggest they grew to value a diverse social network after becoming friends with a broader range of people. One person shared: "I am less interested in making friends with English people and more with international friends." Some volunteers recognized how having diverse friends can help to foster their development. As one volunteer described herself prior to her year: "I was always around the same people, and people my age, it just wasn't developing me." In fact, many volunteers continued to desire friendships with a diverse, international network in college. A volunteer in China, Megan, like many others, reported that she joined the international student society at college and has more "friends who are international students" because of her gap year experience.

In addition to a more diverse social network, volunteers also often cited a growing desire for more *intimate* relationships, especially as they cultivated higher levels of intimacy during their year (e.g., with their volunteer partner or local friends). For instance, Leah shared this: "I desire more intimate relationships now because I can see how much deeper they can go." Further, she said she came to realize that she does not "have the capacity to be intimate with 20 or 30 people; it's not possible. So you have to think carefully about these relationships." Another volunteer, Jenna, echoed this sentiment and said she "had incredibly deep relationships with deep emotions over my year; I want that in university."

Volunteers also became more particular about their friendships as they clarified what they desired in others and the influences others can have on them. One said: "I am now more selective about the people I want to be around . . . and be near me." Another said she now understands herself more and is "more choosy about friends." Leah added that she is "more objective about the impact of relationships" on her, including her "past relationships and how they have influenced [her]." In addition, volunteers seemed to act on these views in college. For example, Dominic, a volunteer in Honduras interviewed in his first year of college, said that, although before his gap year he had had a larger number of "acquaintances," he now has a "smaller group of more intimate friends."

In addition to seeking greater intimacy and placing higher priority on relationships generally, volunteers often came to desire particular traits in people—a particular "wavelength." When I pressed volunteers to articulate what this "wavelength" meant, they generally described an outward-looking and curious orientation toward the world, a desire for adventure and new experiences, and confidence.

Many of the volunteers I interviewed once they were in college were living with other students who also took gap years, which may in part reflect the pull of their interest in these common traits. In the first year, this was facilitated by universities' policies of placing deferred admission students, including gap year students, in the same student building. However, volunteers also reported that "people who took gap years" often "gravitated toward each other" even if they were not assigned to the same housing. Participants said that other gap year students were "interested in many of the same things" and that they felt they could share their "gap year stories with them and they would listen and understand."

Changing Idea of Family

Volunteers widely reported changing ideas of family, often including increased appreciation of its importance. For instance, one volunteer reflected: "In school, doing well in my career is what drove me. But the gap year made me reevaluate my priorities; now I don't know what I want to do, but I do know that it makes family more important for me." Another volunteer in Uganda shared: "I didn't have a close family growing up, but I want that now."

Volunteers' narratives suggest that these changes came from both the felt absence of their own families and immersion in cultures where family is seen as "more important" than in the West. For instance, Megan, a China volunteer, said two years after her experience: "I have more of a family focus because of my year. In the UK, a friend might take care of you when you are ill. In China, ten mothers of friends tried to feed me." One volunteer said: "In Uganda, family focus is more important . . . and I have grown that way too." After his year, another volunteer in Uganda said that he realized that "family is so important—living together—caring for each other." Mark, a volunteer in Chile, said: "The emphasis on closeness to family has increased in my life as being involved in a Chilean family has made me realize that family is extremely important. My time in Chile made me realize how cold and formal British people are in general and that life would be much happier if we all were more caring towards each other."

After living in developing countries where the extended family often plays a larger role than in their home country, several volunteers' understanding of family also broadened to include other relatives. For instance, Leah said that teaching in Namibia "made me want to have a family and kids even more . . . and I saw the importance and gained appreciation of extended family . . . seeing big families in Namibia." Echoing this, a volunteer in Thailand shared: "In the UK people do not appreciate families as much . . . the year made me think about what constitutes a family I thought it was a nuclear family before, but now my understanding is not so rigid; now others can be part of family . . . Thai people became part of my family."

Marriage

Volunteers often changed their views of marriage. Generally, volunteers found that their experiences gave them insight into how marriages can work and some of their practical realities. For instance, one volunteer remarked, "Before my year, I thought really negatively of marriage, but now I see that it is possible to live with one person all the time." Volunteers also reported becoming more realistic about marriage. Leah said that living close to married couples in her community made her realize that "marriages are not all perfect, even Christian marriages . . . I am not as naive now and don't have a delusion about perfect marriages." Realizing the difficulties of maintaining such relationships, one volunteer said: "I have a lot of respect for grandparents—older couples—and how they do it, how they stay together for 25 or 30 years in a marriage. I see my own grandparents and how much they love each other and now I think, what else do you need? I want someone to share all those memories with."

Volunteers also came to seek different qualities in a partner. One said: "It made me think about what type of partner [in marriage] I want. I want someone I can have kids with and have adventures with . . . before I wanted a good career and a good house with kids; now I want someone to have adventures with." After seeing that a relationship with a stranger (her volunteering partner) can work, and the types of relationships she developed overseas with local people, one volunteer reported: "I am more open to the type of person who I might be married to and where I would live. I am also more confident to talk to people I might want a relationship with and in having an international marriage."

Changes in volunteers' view of marriage were, like many others, often also influenced by the local culture. For instance, volunteers in India, a country with a particularly strong focus on family and marriage, experienced changes in their views. After living in a community with arranged marriages, one volunteer said: "Before I thought it was just two people forced to be together—that it was a terrible thing . . . but I realized that marriage is more about compromise, and that arranged marriages can work." She explained how she is "more appreciative of how people can grow to love each other. I also have a more functional interpretation of love; you can grow to love a partner. Sometimes it does not work— but love marriages don't either sometimes." Another volunteer in India said she came to a new understanding of "marriage as an addition to the other person's family; it's about becoming an addition to the family—grandmothers and others included." Similarly, Heather, a volunteer in India, reported, "I didn't want to marry before but now I do; I've seen how important family is, and I want to have a ceremony to officially join families . . . I have a more practical attitude toward marriages and how they can work." Despite growing to be more accepting of these arranged marriages, however, one volunteer in India said these arrangements also made her "appreciate how much freedom we have here in the UK; how we can marry who we love . . . women there have to grow up so fast." Volunteers, especially in India and Uganda, often referenced their experiences with the practice of dowry in helping to shape more "practical" attitudes toward marriage.

Some volunteers also thought that they will be a better spouse because of their gap year experiences, as Leah expressed: "I think I will be a better wife because of my gap year . . . it made me think about what needs to be changed in me to make me a more suitable wife. My gap year helped prepare me for marriage." Likewise, one male volunteer said of his partnership: "It was like a marriage; I will be a better husband because of it. We spent every day together and slept in the same bed for a year."

Children

Some volunteers also changed their view of children after working with them over the year. One female volunteer said: "Before I had a negative view on children—how much responsibility they are, but now I actually like kids; I had a genuine shift in how I view kids; taking care of them can be a real pleasure." Another volunteer changed her mind about having her own children: "Before I didn't want to have children but now I want to have kids. Now I appreciate them, but I want to make sure that I can give them the best life, so I will wait until I am ready." Or another volunteer: "I definitely want to have kids now; I want the responsibility," while one said, "I am now excited to be a mom." Some also said their ideas of who should be involved in the rearing of children changed after their year, as one male volunteer who was in Uganda shared: "In the UK culture you are not supposed to talk to others' kids . . . but now I want to be part of others' children's lives, and I want my children to be involved with more people."

Volunteers also often believed that they would be better parents—and have different parenting strategies—after having to teach and care for children during their gap year. One orphanage volunteer said she "learned how to be a mother." Another said that "being with kids 24/7, you learn how to be a parent" and "how to manage kids." A third said she learned "different parenting techniques;" that while she was initially "yelling and shouting at the kids," she grew to see more "value in parents being confident . . . if you are not confident, kids don't listen."

Other volunteers discussed how they grew to recognize the influence of parenting in a child's life, reporting that they wanted to be, as one volunteer put it, a "role model for [their] children."

Gender Roles

Often, volunteers on their gap year live in cultures with different views of men's and women's proper roles than those that prevail in their home country. Assimilating into the local culture was an opportunity, in many ways, to live the life of another. In this way, volunteers reported a growing awareness and understanding of gender roles, often coming to appreciate the challenges of gender dynamics in other countries, as well as growing to appreciate Western life for women.

In the example below, Margaret, a volunteer in India, discusses the difficulty in "having to become an Indian woman" given the prevailing gender norms there. She outlines the particular challenge of trying to reconcile her life in India and what she experienced now that she is back home:

Having to become an Indian woman was amazing but also the biggest challenge for me I think. I had to live in a way which I feel isn't right. I think women have rights, the right to speak their opinions, to make their own living, to be heard and to make decisions. However in India, this empowerment is only just starting to develop in the area that I lived. I had to gain respect if I wanted to make any friends over there and there are things that women just don't do which I had become used to doing at home, like going out by myself, dressing Western, talking freely whenever and wherever about what I wanted to talk about, speaking to boys and living without someone looking out for me all the time. Some of these things were easy to change and some were very difficult to get my head around.

Harder than feeling repressed myself, was seeing my best friend go from being a fun, chirpy young girl, ready to join in with a water fight or sing songs with me to being a wife at the age of 18. She had to leave and I saw her only once after that, so much skinnier than she was before, sullen and blank as if all the life had disappeared inside her. She was married now to a man who didn't allow her to go back very often to see her family, who was just young himself and had to work hard, who expected her to come in from working in the fields all day and cook and look after him. I spent one horrible evening with her mother and older sister who were distraught after seeing her look so thin and sad. From working in the organization I know that it could have all been much worse, that he could have been a drinker or beaten her or that she could have been much younger. I can see how it all affects villages and how girls get married so young, have lots of children very young and become very weak.

All of this was hard to deal with yet almost harder to look back on now I'm back at home. While I was in India I could understand arranged marriages and I saw a lot of logic in their morals and principles that don't exist over here and it's strange to look back on it.

Volunteers, as seen above, often struggled negotiating the differences between their host country's and more Western perspectives. Another volunteer expressed this, "I was pissed at the status of women there, but felt that it wasn't our place to interfere as volunteers not from China ... women marry men for money more often to escape poverty. It took a lot of tolerance to deal with that."

In another instance, Abigail, a volunteer in Malawi, described adapting to the local culture and its gender roles as her "greatest challenge," "especially the "way women were treated and how they naturally assumed the submissive role in any confrontational situation." Abigail's tensions are illustrated below:

As a woman brought up in a developed country—where equality between sexes is accepted by almost all—it was difficult to accept a submissive role in Malawi just because of my gender. However I learned that just because I must appear submissive did not mean that I had to be, and I did not really have to compromise my lifestyle. Of course a lot of my Malawian friends did understand that women from the West are considered equal to men there, and some even praised that attitude! I also found the forward nature of the men hard to cope with. Men would have no trouble walking straight up to you and asking you to marry them or to give them money and would be insulted if you said "no!" This is a cultural attitude, as I am female they expect me to say "yes" to whatever they demand, even if it is completely unreasonable! However, I learned to cope with this and after a few months I would try and explain to men that it was uncomfortable and unnerving when they wander up to me and demand marriage!

Many female volunteers left their gap year with a greater appreciation of gender equality in the West. One volunteer said: "I now appreciate the greater gender equality we have in the UK." But some volunteers also came to appreciate how conservative gender roles can help society function by dividing labor.

Male volunteers also expressed changes in their views on gender roles. Some reported feeling frustrated or resistant to adopting a local custom as the dominant gender. Dan, a volunteer in Uganda said: "When women would bow to me in Uganda, I hated it . . . it really pissed me off." In another situation, a volunteer said he developed an appreciation of how men can contribute to domestic duties from his time in Guyana. He said: "I came home and I was pissed at my dad and brother for not helping around the house—in Guyana men in my area helped."

Relationships with People Back Home

Family of Origin

It is not surprising that, given these changing conceptions of family, almost all volunteers described changes—typically improvements—in their relationships with their families of origin as a result of their gap year.

Outlining these "improved" relationships, volunteers reported changing dynamics as parents shifted away from a parent-child relationship to ones built more on mutual respect as competent adults. One volunteer mentioned this change: "It was hard for my mom to let her child go to China . . . it changed our relationship . . . to more of a friendship." Another volunteer in China, Megan, said: "Before my year, my dad said it was a waste of time. He said to get a job; don't go to university; that I should work. It was hard fundraising without their support." However, she reported, "When I came back, I didn't have an 18-year-old teenage relationship with parents—my patience had been tried so much over the year that my parents didn't bother me—I was much more easy going. They treated me like an adult—not saying 'when are you coming home?' Or 'It's bed time.'" Another volunteer shared this: "Over my year I saw my mom in myself—how much we are like each other. I used to get so irritated at her; now I just laugh at her . . . we understand each other much more now; she does not annoy me anymore . . . our relationship has certainly improved . . . my mum treats me more as an adult now and gives me leeway."

Volunteers often cited concrete evidence of this changed relationship. Dominic, a South Africa volunteer, said that he engaged in new behavior around the house: "Why was I such a dick before? Before I used to give such a hard time to my parents—when they asked me to do something, like empty the dishwasher, I wouldn't do it and I gave them such a hard time." After coming back from his year, Dominic said: "I help out around the house much more now . . . I empty the dishwasher when I get home—either she or I have to do it. Why should it be her? She has been working so hard all day to support me—and I had been doing dishes all my gap year."

Another returned volunteer described her parents' surprise when she came home after her year and helped prepare dinner and clean afterward, saying it felt so "natural to help." Because of her gap year, she said she now understood how "much work it takes to run a household." A volunteer in Japan echoed this: "My family relations really improved after my year. I really appreciate what my parents do with three kids now . . . I help with dishes and cleaning now . . . I had to do the dishes myself all year."

Negotiating the changing relationship between parents and volunteers can sometimes be contentious. Returning home with increased feelings of independence, many described tension when parents reverted to being their children's caretakers and monitors. Robert felt this way after a year in Uganda: "When your parents ask when you are coming home and what are you doing . . . it is bothersome since you've been living alone for so long."

However, not all family relationships improve during the gap year. For instance, Jennie, a volunteer who spent her year in the Dominican Republic who we met in chapter 2, said:

> My relationship with my father became worse because of my year. Our relationship was bad before and he did not support me going overseas. Like the day I left, my father just came to the edge of the stairs, and said, "okay, bye." During my year we didn't talk . . . I only called him once on his birthday.

After coming back from her year, Jennie reported: "I said I wanted to go out, but my father said no. He was trying to control me like a child, so I left and moved in with a friend for week and got away from him."

Volunteers' narratives suggest a number of reasons for improved family relationships over the year, especially missing their families of origin, having to care for themselves and for children during the year and appreciating more the role that families can play. One volunteer said: "I had a bad teenage relationship with my parents . . . but it got much better after the year away . . . it's a lot of hassle looking after someone. Over my year I had a full-time job—I had to budget money—take care of myself—it just made me realize how much effort [parents] put into you. They work so hard to take care of me." Working with children and families in her gap year country, one volunteer said: "I appreciate what my parents did to stay active in my life." The importance of family in many of the local cultures also played a role. For instance, a volunteer in China said: "There is a big importance of family there. It helped me to see how much my family in the UK means . . . how happy they make you and how much comfort they are."

Simply being away from family also seemed to help these relationships in many cases. Dominic, for example, said his relationship with his parents improved because he was "away from [his] family for the first time—and we just had time apart, so we didn't argue about stupid stuff, daily things—we just talked once in a while—and just talked without arguing." Being overseas and away from family during the gap year often removed many of the sources of disagreement between volunteers and their parents. Further, volunteers often cited the adage that "absence makes the heart grow fonder," recalling how they missed their families over the year. Leah's absence from her family made them less habituated to her presence when she returned: "There is a novelty now . . . my parents smile when I walk in. My presence is really enjoyed with my parents now."

Some volunteers said the "support" their parents and siblings offered overseas also helped to improve their relationships. Interestingly, some felt that the context of the gap year allowed them to "open up" to their parents more emotionally and share with them than they had before. One volunteer said that coming back, she was surprised to go back and read the "letters to my parents that I wrote over the year . . . I really opened up to them. I was surprised; they were really personal." Leah said that she had an "emotional year where she dealt with personal issues, but she shared them with her parents through letters." Ironically, it was often the distance that seemed central to improving communications in these relationships. As seen in the gap year context, sometimes being away and talking less created spaces for more deep communication.

Friends

Volunteers described how their friendships in their home countries changed as a result of the gap year, often owing to the volunteers' new priorities or perspectives. Although some volunteers said they kept many of the same friends before and after the year—during which these friends were supportive—volunteers more often reported "losing" friends or having different opinions of them upon their return. Sometimes, just the fact that the person was away from their home community changed their relationships with their friends: "You learn who your real friends are when you are on your gap year . . . who is actually going to put the effort in to communicate and maintain the relationships, to support you too." Another volunteer shared a similar experience, "When I went away, I had a massive leaving party, but over the year I only missed 4 or 5 of them."

Volunteers mentioned that they came to seek different qualities in friends, which affected their friendships from home. One said: "My friends in the UK are so wasteful; it's really frustrating because they don't care; they don't want to travel; they gossip. Things seem so trivial with them; I didn't stay friends with many of them." These changes can pose challenges on the volunteers' return. One shared: "Coming back I had no place among my friends, but I realized that they are doing the same thing as before, going to the same pub and drinking, and I didn't miss anything. You feel a bit smug, snobby—you feel culturally different." Likewise, a Thailand volunteer said: "Coming back, all my friends seemed boring. All they want to talk about is hair and makeup and gossip and I don't care about that anymore."

Male and female volunteers both commented on how their friends cared about issues they no longer saw as important and had perspectives on issues that they no longer shared. Often, these changes were discerned when people returned from their gap year and saw differences in how they were from their peers. One volunteer reported that this process of learning about how the gap year changed him continued into his second year of college as situations arose where he "saw how [he] was different" from his peers.

Romantic Relationships

It was almost universal that romantic relationships between a gap year volunteer and their significant other back home ended during the gap year or ended preemptively before the year began. Often volunteers said they "grew apart" or that the "long distance" was too much because of lack of communication and interaction, or that after some months into the year the volunteer realized that their boyfriend or girlfriend "didn't share the same interests," as one participant put it. However, I was able to identify and interview one volunteer who stayed together with her boyfriend over the year. She said they "called daily" and "worked hard at staying in touch" and that they have a stronger relationship now" after she came back. However, another volunteer whose partner had a relationship that survived the whole year said that during her year her partner often "had to leave friends to take a call from the UK . . . and it prevented her from getting more out of her year, having a really great year." Volunteers, as has been mentioned in other sections, often expressed that immersion in the local culture, without constant communication with home country, was critical to learning and changing from the gap year, a subject that we will come back to at greater length in chapters 6, 7, and 8.

Somewhat frequently, volunteers developed romantic relationships with local men or women in their gap year communities or had sexual relations with fellow travelers during their vacations. Some volunteers said that their desire to learn about the local culture led them to start a relationship with a local man or woman.

Female volunteers who did have romantic relationships with local men often gave a variety of reasons for having done so. Reduced worries about "reputation" while overseas away from home and the "attention" females received from local men were discussed, among other motives, as reasons for sexual activity overseas. However, sometimes these female volunteers regretted these relationships, realizing, as one volunteer said, that "he wanted me for a trophy; I just didn't see it." Romantic relationships, especially ones involving sexual relations, can be a significant risk in gap years, especially when they are contrary to local customs and involve unprotected sex.

Some people stated that they had changed their opinion of the attractiveness of local people over time or had developed an interest, or even a preference, for people from the area. Oliver, a volunteer in Bolivia, recalled that upon arrival he did not think the women were attractive there, but one day, about halfway through his year, went out and thought: "Did a bus full of good-looking girls just arrive?" These changes seemed to be long-lasting for some volunteers. Some participants in college reported a continued desire to date males or females with ethnic origins in the volunteer's gap year country (e.g., Hispanic or Chinese), sometimes exclusively dating those of a particular ethnicity while in college.

Analysis

As this chapter's narratives illustrate, the gap year changed how volunteers saw themselves and their relationships with others.

For many volunteers, this change was not just a process of self-clarification—individuation—but also a realization of the importance of living in community. Thus, a key theme emerging from these findings is a general move toward incorporating others into one's life, being "others-oriented" in a way that others become more recognized and important. Reflecting this, Robert White (1981) suggested that students who are engaged in volunteering may magnify their humanitarian concern. He defined this as "behavior directed toward the good of others but also the feelings that prompt such behavior" and hypothesized that whatever level of altruism they began with would probably expand. My findings support White's hypothesis. Moreover, research has identified that having an orientation toward others and feeling connected with others improve subjective well-being and community life (Baumeister et al. in press; Putnam 2000). This connection will be discussed further in the next chapter on civic and religious changes.

What I learned from interviewing the students is also consistent with early studies in service learning, which found changes in terms of participants' concern or care for others (Kahne and Westheimer 1999; Kellogg 1999; Kiely 2004). The data in my study indicated that volunteers developed deeper levels of care and understanding of others' well-being through their professional roles and by building relationships with others, generally corroborating Robert Rhoads's (1997) finding that service-learning courses promoted caring attitudes. My findings are also supported by recent research showing that empathy-related parts of the brain, like muscles, can be developed as people use them more often, especially when placed in new social contexts (Kim 2010). Further, an improved ability (e.g., empathy, communication skills) and desire to interact with others (e.g. tolerance, social confidence) have also been noted in other studies of service learning and study abroad (e.g., Eyler and Giles 1999; Kauffmann et al. 1992).

In a similar vein, these gap years often placed men in caretaking roles in social care and teaching, which seemed to help foster "empathy," "compassion" and "patience" in some of them. As John Dalton (1988) argues, in the West, fulfilling expectations of masculinity can make it difficult for men to display vulnerability, to express care and nurturance in relationships, and to admit uncertainty and need for assistance. Carol Gilligan (1982) also believes that men develop less fully in the areas of empathy, caring, and nurturance because they have been socialized to view these attributes as less important. Ursula Delworth and David Seeman (1984) make much the same point in arguing that male development centers on autonomy and only later on intimacy. From male volunteers' accounts, the gap year seems to give them caretaking roles and opportunities earlier in life, in a context that nourishes such capacities as "empathy" and "care."

As these interpersonal changes occurred, volunteers reported that relationships changed with those around them and in their home countries, including their parents. Although there is little previous work on this topic, some researchers have found that U.S. students' relationships with their parents generally improve during study abroad, while romantic relationships and friendships suffer (Kauffmann et al. 1992; Uehara 1986).

The narratives examined here suggest that many of these interpersonal changes occurred as volunteers' sense of themselves was challenged. Building relationships with a wider range of people during their gap year (compared with their lives before) also seemed to help volunteers imagine new possible relationships, interactions, and ways of being. As volunteers were integrated into their gap year community, they found themselves more able to take on others' perspectives, which affected how they viewed people different from themselves. Their narratives suggest that they became more comfortable with difference and more understanding, open, and tolerant. David Siegel (2010) also observed this relationship in his research on mindfulness, finding that interacting with others allows us to better understand ourselves. He writes: "As we grow in our ability to know ourselves, we become receptive to knowing each other" (2010, 231).

The experiences that I studied support recent research on social networks and college students' cognitive and moral development. W. Pitt Derryberry and Stephen Thoma (2000) found that students with more diverse social networks (and thus more exposure to different ways of understanding the world) typically had greater cognitive and moral development than did those with more homogenous networks. Often during adolescence, young people spend a considerable amount of time exclusively with people their own age (Csikszentmihalyi et al. 1977), but the gap year environment seemed to provide—and encourage—greater interaction with a diverse range of ages.

In review, volunteers' narratives suggest that their experiences over their gap year helped change their understandings of interpersonal issues (e.g., of family, of romance). Findings also suggest that these experiences may have helped them to develop a greater capacity to understand others and to have a deeper disposition to consider others' interests. In the next chapter, we examine how the gap year affects students in the civic and religious spheres.

4

Changes in Religious and Civic Perceptions

Religion

Gap year experiences frequently had an impact on the way volunteers view religion. Volunteers were often in developing countries and in rural locations where religiosity is high and where there are often religions other than the one they are most accustomed to. Away from their home communities and encountering foreign religious traditions, many volunteers had their understanding of religion challenged over their gap year. The impacts are not uniform, and, as seen below, volunteers responded differently to similar experiences.

For some, simply being in a different environment changed their understanding of their own religious beliefs: One volunteer recalled that early in her year she realized that she didn't have a desire to go to church and that, even though she "had gone to church all [her] life, it was only because [her] family went."

Many volunteers said that they lost their faith or that the gap year at least amplified their religious doubts. Some volunteers said this occurred as a result of living in poverty or witnessing injustice and not being able to reconcile this with their concept of God. For instance, after hearing about the rape of one of the orphans in her care, one volunteer found herself asking: "How could God let this happen?" In other cases, it was conversion practices or perceived corruption in the local church that changed participants' views. For instance, Mark, a volunteer in Uganda, claims that his year "turned me off to religion." He recalled:

> In our Ugandan village people preached to us all the time. They would come to our house asking, "Don't you want to be saved?" And they always were trying to convince us with the same creator argument. They would say things like, "Look

at this chair; it has a creator—so do you and the world must too." It turned us off to religion. At the church service the pastor would say things like, "If you give money to the church then god will give you back more in life." It was corrupt.

In another example, one volunteer reported that the "missionaries there were very dogmatic and really negative . . . they were really strict and rigid . . . and it turned me off."

Other volunteers said it was interacting with foreign and unfamiliar religious practices, such as exorcisms, and the justifications offered for these that accelerated their doubts or loss of faith during their year. Martha, a volunteer in rural Chile, remembered one particular instance where she felt distanced from religion: "There was one time they had three priests performing an exorcism on a little girl; they wanted to drive the evil spirits out, but all she had was a temper tantrum."

However, experiences over the year also strengthened volunteers' faith or even led to conversion. While one volunteer was "turned off" by missionaries, a few reported that experiences and interactions with missionaries over the year inspired them to convert to Christianity. Michelle, who spent her year working in an orphanage in Peru, said she learned "more about Christianity in my gap year than in [her] entire 20 years of life." Both she and her gap year partner converted to Christianity and were baptized during their time in Peru. Leah, a volunteer who spent her year in Namibia teaching that we met in chapter 2, suggested that her Christian faith was strengthened by the new challenges posed by her gap year. She explained:

> When I went out there, I didn't know people to rely on; I was stripped of social support—God was the only foundation I had out there to see me through, and I had to rely on faith. And God spoke to me in new and exciting ways over my year. I worked in a Christian school, and there was a strong Christian community fellowship. I made friends with older people who were more spiritually mature—I got bogged down in teenage issues and they brought me up and offered new insight.

While some people's experiences with poverty and injustice amplified their doubts about religion, Leah grew stronger in her faith because she "saw how God blessed us when we were working for others." Some other volunteers recalled that the additional time for reading and thinking about religion allowed by their gap year strengthened their faith.

Regardless of developments in their own personal faiths, many volunteers reported a greater understanding and appreciation both of religion, generally, and of the particular religions represented in their gap year communities. Although some were disenchanted with religious institutions they viewed as corrupt, volunteers also frequently described an increased appreciation of the role that religion can play in enriching and sustaining personal and community life. One said that after his gap year in Uganda he does not "dismiss religion like I used to." Another who volunteered in Guyana said he realized in a new way that "religion can be a massive part of people's lives."

Ben, who worked in an outdoor education school in South Africa, said that his position as the instructor "forced" him to "deal with religious issues" and accommodate interfaith differences. Because Muslim students in his group had to wash themselves and pray in foreign ways, Ben recalled thinking: "Why do they believe this? How can I help integrate this? I learned I need to make time for people to pray, and I got the group to help them find northeast to Mecca to pray." He observed that, "when you have friends and colleagues of other faiths, it makes you appreciate and understand why people of other faiths do things." In particular, he recalled "learning that you can't force a Muslim to accept Christianity, and you can't segregate." Ben said that now he hopes to "promote understanding in my home community between races and religions" by exposing people to their misconceptions about those of other races or faiths.

Community

Volunteers' ideas of "community" often evolved as a result of their experiences, especially if they were located in small rural areas. Many volunteers suggested that the substantial duration of their stays in their host communities enabled them to become highly "integrated" there and that this sense of belonging, of "home," offered an avenue to grow in understanding themselves, their home communities, and the type of community they want in the future.

Volunteers often felt increasingly integrated into the community as they came to understand the culture's dynamics throughout the four seasons of the year. One volunteer who lived in an aboriginal village in the rainforest in Guyana said: "I changed because I lived as a local. I saw the world from a villager's perspective. I could have found a wife and stayed there—I was at that level." Or Jess, a volunteer in India: "I became so integrated into the small Indian community that I felt at home and a part of it." Another volunteer said that the "novelty is stimulating, novelty grabs you, it really excites you. You get into the culture . . . and develop your sense of community—then you can really understand the culture—and you gain new perspectives; you can understand yourself and the UK better."

Volunteers commonly recalled discovering the pleasures of community life during their year. Mark, a volunteer in rural Honduras, said:

> Life over there is very different and I had to adapt to a very different culture in order to fit in. But the fact is I did that and I became Teacher Mark . . . I enjoyed being part of somewhere completely different, not just being there, but actually being an active member of the community. I had my house, my students, my friends, my job, my hangouts and it was a whole new life for a year. I enjoy the fact that I was able to call such an idyllic place home for a year and have the privilege to be accepted by the people over there.

Similarly, a volunteer in Uganda said: "The sense of community I get from my project is awesome, and I love being a part of it."

People often left their gap year with a conception of and desire for community life that is more active and intimate than they had previously known. Another Uganda volunteer said he grew to "appreciate the value in community, where people are interested in each other and care about each other." Kyle, a volunteer in a small town in Guyana, said: "There was a real sense of community; everyone was working together for our community. It made me realize that in the UK, people are born into individualism, to think about themselves first rather than the community." Kyle added:

> Now when I see people in cities back in UK wearing jerseys for football teams and chanting for their city, I sometimes think that they often don't really do anything to contribute to those communities. . . . I have an enthusiasm now about being part of civil society and for life in general that I have brought back with me in the UK. . . . Before Guyana I used to think about what I can get from society, but now I think about what I can give to society.

Two weeks before school started, Kyle had already signed up for a student volunteering society in his college. Similarly, Ryan, a Uganda volunteer, said: "It was really nice to know my neighbors overseas . . . Before I was a citizen at the base level, but my year taught me more of what it meant to be a good citizen—that you have a responsibility to the people you are surrounded by."

Volunteers stressed the pleasure of feeling a part of the community so often that I was curious to discover why they valued this aspect of their experience so highly. They offered a range of different answers. Some emphasized the novelty of the experience and the sense that they had never felt so "active" or "needed" in a community before. Others described a special satisfaction that came from making a strange place familiar, after having being stripped of their home and support network at the outset of the year. Several volunteers also felt that their emotional connection to the community—and the pleasure they drew from it—were due to the fact that they had invested in the community and contributed to others there, as well as receiving much in return. One volunteer said: "I gave to the community, and I received a bunch back, so you feel grateful—connected—and you want to give more."

Volunteers often compared their attachment to their home with the sense of community they developed overseas. One said that because of her year, she came to find it "strange not to know your neighbors in the UK. Before I went I didn't care that I didn't know them. I would have said of course I don't know them. But it's creepy; it's terrible that I don't know my neighbors. I sleep 10 meters from them. I don't want that type of neighborhood." More broadly, volunteers were often disappointed by the lack of "community" or "friendliness" they encountered upon their return.

Some changed their minds about where they want to live in their home country as a result. One volunteer who had grown up in the suburbs of Glasgow said: "I wanted to live in a city before—I thought there would be more opportunities and it would be more exciting—but now I want to live somewhere rural because there is a greater sense of community there." Many volunteers who entered universities upon their return also reported trying to foster community on campus.

Volunteers in urban and rural placements often had very different experiences of community. Volunteers in cities, especially those who lived and worked in an orphanage, generally felt less integrated into their communities and developed a more limited sense of the wider social environment. This more limited integration often meant that volunteers were not influenced and challenged in ways that others were.

For example, Tobias suggested that his gap year in Santiago, Chile, did not do enough to spur him to develop relationships or integrate into a community. He explained:

I wasn't sure how I wanted to change from my gap year—I just thought change would be good. I didn't like going out in the UK—I just thought that going out in Chile would be different. I wanted to have to do things I wouldn't do, but I wasn't forced to do things I wouldn't do enough. I wanted to become more extroverted but I wasn't forced . . . Yeah, I talked to teachers and socialized . . . but you can still be anonymous there . . . There are so many pressures in cities to stay quiet, to not share. People are not as open in cities—they are often individuals not interested in how others are doing. So there is a pressure to be quiet—to go on with your own business. I had my [host] family there—and friends—but not really a sense of community.

Another volunteer in Japan recalled that when the gap year provider asked him to write a report about his local community, he said that he "didn't really have that." This sentiment was echoed by other volunteers in large cities, who were "disappointed" that they didn't have the same "opportunities to get involved" as their peers did in more rural locations. After comparing her experiences with other participants, one volunteer who lived in a rural town in Chile went as far as suggesting that gap year providers "shouldn't send people to cities." "You have so much more opportunity to get involved in small communities," she said as she proudly shared pictures of herself as a firefighter in her town.

To be sure, entering a rural community also has its challenges. One volunteer found her small community "claustrophobic" at times, and another felt "naked" as the object of staring and gossip in hers. Overall, however, volunteers who were placed in rural environments were much more likely to have felt an increased appreciation for community life than those who were placed in cities, and this was seen as a source of special value by those participants who experienced it.

Moral Dilemmas

Gap year experiences often presented volunteers with situations that challenged their moral commitments and forced them to grapple with novel dilemmas. For instance, volunteers working as teachers were often urged by school leaders, fellow teachers, and parents to use corporal punishment. Participants weighed their own opposition to this practice against their desire to meet the expectations of the community, with most but not all refusing to hit their students.

Will explained that a "gap year of greater duration makes you come into contact with situations which are in conflict with moral positions. . . . Over my year I came into contact with all these moral situations—treatment of the mentally handicapped, corporal punishment—but over time I realized and understood from their perspective why they are like that or why they do that." "In the end," he said, "it clarified my moral judgments and moral values." Like Will, many volunteers reported that their own moral views did not change fundamentally in light of their experiences, but that they nonetheless developed a greater understanding of why a culture or community might see morality differently than they do.

Others, however, did describe feeling unsure about some of their own moral convictions after their year. As one put it, "I had clear ideas about morality before, but my year messed them up." Another explained: "Before, I thought, 'Oh no, stealing, that is really wrong.' But then someone actually stole some money from me. 'Well,' I thought, 'maybe that person may actually really need that money.'" This volunteer described herself as transitioning from a "black and white" view of morality to a "gray" one that is more situational and context-based. Likewise, Ryan said his encounters with bribery in Uganda helped him to see that morality has a relative dimension and is "less cut and dry." Regardless, volunteers often moved to a greater ability to assess moral situations because they took context into consideration more. Tom, a volunteer in Guyana, illustrates: "I'm more able to understand culture without saying 'they believe in this and this is bad, and that is against my beliefs, so it is bad.' Now I can be more objective about it and say that is a belief, and this is why they believe this and it has come from this, rather than just automatically judging it."

Volunteers also handled the tensions between their own moral views and the expectations of their communities in different ways. Asked how she reacted to the use of corporal punishment, one volunteer in Bolivia said: "You become desensitized to it over time—it's part of everyday life." Similarly, another volunteer, in Uganda, suggested that "eventually you get used to it and the country and don't think that much about it. You have to put it off—if you don't then you will be affected." However, others said that they remained sensitive to what they perceived as brutality, but that they endeavored to manage this reaction in other ways. As one put it, "You don't really become desensitized to it—not really. Rather, you make it relative to the country." Volunteers who did not actively process the moral dissonance they experienced at the time often find that it became a lingering source of difficulty for them upon returning to their home country. I discuss this phenomenon in chapter 5.

In some cases, volunteers actually adopted and internalized particular moral norms or customs prevalent in their host communities. One female volunteer said that after her gap year in a conservative Muslim community, "I cover myself more. I always cover my ankles now." Similarly, a male volunteer, two years after his experience abroad, said: "I am more conservative in my dress. I don't care about the temperature; I never wear shorts in public."

More broadly, many volunteers described how their exposure to maltreatment of others made abstract moral issues more salient in their daily lives. Sara, a volunteer in a school in Honduras, said: "The school provides a safe haven for the children; some are beaten at home, some are fearful of their fathers, of the belt. Some sleep in a dark room on the floor with cockroaches. They are abused; no child should have to go through this." Volunteers often struggled to reconcile their awareness of the adversity of others' lives with their own relative privilege. Lucy, a volunteer in an orphanage in Cambodia, recalled her own experience:

> Five children died during my time in Cambodia, and the news of the deaths always hit me hard. There was one experience in particular where we attended the funeral. I was struck by its simplicity and felt numb and disorientated for days. I cried for her, for her grandmother and for the system. There was nothing available in the country to save her. It was heartbreaking. She had led such a short life and to me that just didn't seem fair. Although those times were tough I dealt with the emotional struggles by looking forward and focusing on the children that were still with us. Dealing with sick children in the hospital also used to be a big challenge. Seeing them on the verge of death because of a virus that had taken control of their body was so hard. It frustrated me that Western countries live SO differently from countries like Cambodia.

Toby, a volunteer in Bolivia, wrote during his year of returning to his group house after "sit[ting] under a dark bridge with a man dying of TB and HIV" and experiencing "an irrational hate towards the sound of laughter coming from the lounge." Toby said that he aims to "see the humanity in what we do, even if it may seem futile in most instances."

Poverty and International Development

Living in communities and developing relationships with local people, volunteers often encountered the implications of poverty and structural inequalities on a very personal level. For instance, one volunteer said: "Living in this community for a year has opened my eyes to problems such as poverty and education." This awareness triggered changes in the ways volunteers understood poverty, social problems, and ways to improve them.

After living in a developing community on the same wages as most local people, volunteers often shifted to a more relative view of poverty that appreciates a diversity of ways of living. For example, one Guyana volunteer said: "I think my idea of poverty became more relative. Before I thought, they don't have running water; that is really terrible; people are suffering—but it is just a different way of life." Mark, a volunteer in an aboriginal village in Guyana's rain forest said: "Poverty? Before my year I thought they were poor, but they are not poor! They live in the rain forest and have all their possessions in the rain forest—if they need something they go and get it there."

At the same time, volunteers' new perspectives of ways of being also caused them to feel a tension between international development and preserving a way of life. Mark's change caused him to question the direction of development: "It just challenges the idea of what they are developing to? To be like the UK?" Leah, a volunteer in Namibia, also reported this tension between development and preserving a way of life: "I struggled to draw the line—to help them without wiping out local culture . . . like, in Namibia they have lots of kids that they can't afford. I wanted to impose a Western view on them—the same with sexism and abuse there. I wanted to yell that it is wrong, but that is from the developed world."

It is also apparent that volunteers often began to broaden the way they looked at social problems. This shift was particularly visible in their views of international aid, especially when volunteers were in locations that had large amounts of foreign charity. Even though many grew in their desire to help others in developing countries, volunteers reported becoming more skeptical of aid organizations and international development during their gap year—they came to appreciate the challenges and complexities of social and political problems. Further, volunteers often shifted to appreciate a more "grassroots," culturally relevant, and community-based orientation to social change.

People frequently experienced inefficiencies, misdirection, and culturally inappropriate approaches to international aid as sources of this shift. For instance, Jessica, a volunteer in India, spoke about her increasing skepticism of international development, but also felt that long-term immersion provides good insight into how to improve it:

> I also realized that developing countries can not only be helped with money
> or things like that. Problems that occur are very structural and often based in
> centuries old ways of thinking. Often help is not given in the right way or even
> by the right people and because of that it hardly reaches its goal. The way that

help is given is more important than what help is given. It will only reach its goal if you look from the receiving country's perspective, not from the giving country. And that's difficult, because that's where cultural misunderstandings come in again. Can a Western person ever understand the way of thinking of an Indian? I don't know, but I do know that living in a country and really being part of community definitely gives you a step in the good direction.

Another volunteer in India, Helen, echoed the need for culturally relevant aid after returning from her gap year:

I now see that aid is continually misguided. For example, child sponsorship schemes are spending almost more on administration than on improving the child's well-being. I think positive change can only come through education relevant to people's needs. This type of assistance will create self-reliant and proud communities better able to assert their rights.

Eileen described how a charity misdirected its aid:

A Dutch charity would send these boxes down and they were totally inappropriate, full of sports equipment and things the children didn't need.

John shared his thoughts on how his opinion of Ugandan people changed his orientation to development on a fundamental level:

Before I left for my year, I thought that Ugandans were helpless people trying to make a living out of nothing, but by the end I really didn't like some of the people, and it made me view them as capable people, just like any community; that they actually do have a fairly large modicum of control over their lives, and they can make changes; it's just a long-term process.

Another volunteer in Uganda, Rob, demonstrated his simultaneous increase in commitment to helping others with an increased skepticism of international aid and a shift to a local approach to development:

I am the charity officer for the student council at my college, but the value I have of charity is a lot less. I am not against charity now; I just don't attach much value to things like international charities. I really felt by the end that Ugandan problems can only be solved by Ugandan people.

In a response to this growing skepticism of outside aid, many volunteers said that in donating to charities, they now prefer charities that are embedded in the community and understand the needs of the people and dynamics of the local culture.

Materialism

Volunteers' experiences often influenced their views of material goods. Often, volunteers moved away from the more materialistic orientations that are associated with the developed world toward an increased appreciation of immaterial pursuits (e.g. relationships with others, community, helping others), especially after being in an environment that valued immaterial goods more than their place of origin.

For instance, a volunteer interviewed three years after her stay in northwest China described her changing priorities away from materialism: "I had a real change in priorities from my gap year. Things that were important before aren't anymore, like before I had to have a new dress every weekend before I went out drinking—and now I don't care about that." One volunteer recalled that he "didn't realize how materialistic [he] was before his year . . . that [he] always wanted new clothes or technology" but it changed after his year. David, a volunteer in Uganda, explained that after confronting poverty during his year, he realized he "took things for granted" in his life. He recalled: "I realized that life isn't about the material things but about the people who are in your life."

Volunteers gave a number of reasons for this. Some thought having the opportunity to live without very many material possessions and within a community of friends and people that had little—but were happy—moved them to question their own orientation to material goods and appreciate a life with less. An India volunteer said: "I don't think material possessions are as important as they were before. I now realize that having a tiny house does not mean you are unhappy, and neither does a lack of shoes." A volunteer in the Dominican Republic stated:

> I gained a new outlook on the important things in life. It was so humbling to see how little some people had in their homes but yet how willing they were to invite us in and share their food or simply the warmth of their company with us. It taught me that living simply with less possessions and less worries actually does make you happier. It helped me enjoy and appreciate the simple things in life."

Or another volunteer in Honduras who said:

> I realized I don't need copious amounts of stuff; I just need enough to get by. In the West having so much choice can be tiring and not necessarily a good thing;

people can be happy with the very basic. Although some would view the house we lived in as poor to me it had everything I needed, and actually for that year, that I wanted.

Often, volunteers grew to have negative views of a materialistic orientation in their home country and priorities of people there. A volunteer who spent her year in an orphanage in Peru said: "I see so many more flaws with our society than I did before. I feel despair with the lifestyle choices made by people including me and the amount of time we waste on insignificant things, and the amount of money we spend on things we don't need—people's obsession with wealth and constantly needing things they don't really need."

Volunteers also cited a growing recognition of poverty and inequality in the world as justification for a shift away from materialism. Abigail, a volunteer in Malawi, reported, "I feel now that there are a lot more important things to consider than whether I should buy a new top or not, or whether I should have done my homework! There are so many huge issues in the world where people should be helping others less fortunate but many people in the UK seem to be unaware of these!" Megan, the volunteer in China cited above, elucidates how the gap year—and the issues of poverty—caused her to question her priorities:

> The year makes you question your beliefs—why we are the way we are; why we do the things that we do. We get fancy jobs to make lots of money to buy lots of things, just things. And because you have so much responsibility in your job overseas, and the issues you are dealing with there make these things seem trivial. You live with people who are so hard working and have much less and they are happier—you just see these thing as trivial, as materialism.

Many volunteers, even long after their gap year, became more economical, often reporting reduced consumption and evaluating products (e.g., clothes, technology) based on "need" rather than "want." One volunteer captured this: "Now when I go to the store I ask, "Do I just want this, or do I actually need this?""

Analysis

In this chapter on civic and religious perceptions, the experiences of gap year volunteers show how living and engaging in settings of cultural difference often altered their understandings of community, religion, education, and poverty and civic affairs, as well as their relation to them. Exposure to new ways of understanding and making meaning of the world prompted this for many volunteers.

In Jack Mezirow's (2000) terminology, participants' narratives suggest that their understandings of the world that were "uncritically assimilated" from their childhood were challenged.

With regard to community, volunteers seemed to alter the conceptions of community that they had assimilated from their home culture and way of living, often developing more active conceptions of it. Stronger and different notions of community life were noted among those in rural communities, patterns also seen by social scientists who suggest that major urban areas tend to have less community ties, less civic engagement, and lower social capital. As Robert Putnam (2000, 206) writes:

> The resident of a major metropolitan area is significantly less likely to attend
> public meetings, to be active in community organizations, to attend church, to
> sign a petition, to volunteer, to attend club meetings, to work on community
> projects, or even to visit friends. Metropolitans are less engaged because of where
> they are, not who they are . . . Living in a major metropolitan agglomeration
> somehow weakens civic engagement and social capital."

Mark Twain (1867) made a similar observation of New York City in a letter to the newspaper *Alta California*: "It is a splendid desert—a doomed and steepled solitude, where a stranger is lonely in the midst of a million of his race." As Luis Roser-Bixby et al. (2005, 5) observe in their study of demographic trends in Latin America: "It is paradoxical that close proximity and high population density of cities have decreased, instead of increasing, the density of social connections."

Although research has not deeply examined the role of educational interventions in developing individuals' orientations toward community life, a more participatory attitude toward community is suggested in service-learning literatures (e.g., Eyler and Giles 1999). Furthermore, Jenifer McGuire and Wendy Gamble's (2006) study of domestic volunteering found that participants had increases in their feelings of community belonging and social responsibility. In their study, psychological engagement, not number of hours spent, accounted for significant variability in participants' attitudes about community. The intensity of psychological engagement seems to be especially high in this study's gap year participants, an issue that will be covered in more depth in chapter 7.

Similarly, volunteers sometimes altered their conceptions of morality after encountering moral dilemmas. As volunteers encountered difference, such as new ways of punishment, they reported that they tried to fit these concepts into existing moral frameworks. Engaging with this difference sometimes resulted in volunteers altering their moral positions. More important, however, is that their narratives suggest that they moved toward more relative ways of evaluating moral dilemmas—moving away from dualistic positions of right and wrong. In other words, attempts to make meaning of new dissonant experiences seemed to promote movement toward the capacities for more complex ways of making meaning. In the case of religion, this engagement in difference often resulted in new religious perspectives. Like with moral dilemmas, through living in the communities, empathy, and imagination on behalf of the volunteers, it seems that they attempted to make meaning from a local perspective, thereby developing an appreciation of the role that religion can play in sustaining personal and community life.

Volunteers' shift away from materialistic values seems important to their personal and public lives. Kasser (2002) found that when people have more materialistic values (e.g., value being wealthy and having many possessions), they report less happiness and life satisfaction—and have weaker interpersonal relationships and contribute less to the community. At the same time, volunteers' corresponding growing desire for relationships and social connectedness from the gap year is also likely to increase volunteers' well-being and community life later. John Helliwell and Robert Putnam (2004, 1435) found that social connections "all appear independently and robustly related to happiness and life satisfaction, both directly and through their impact on health."

In addition, this chapter showed ways that living in developing communities also altered volunteers' ways of understanding poverty and their relationship to it, with many volunteers developing more sophisticated and nuanced understandings. This supports Richard Kiely's (2004) supposition of changed conceptions of poverty through an international service-learning experience, although the magnitude and the depth of understanding of international development and culture may be noticeably higher in a gap year due to its extended duration and immersion.

Experiences of gap year volunteers also partially rebuts Kate Simpson's (2004) claim that—because gap year provider organizations do not provide participants with an explicit social justice perspective (e.g., academic and pedagogical resources) and rely solely on experience for an education—volunteers develop simplistic and crude understandings of different cultures and do not engage critically with international development issues. On the contrary, I found that an international volunteering gap year program with a structured, long-term placement that encourages integration can help participants develop more sophisticated understandings of international development and culture without an explicit social justice frame. In fact, participants often developed quite skeptical attitudes toward international development.

Even without the explicit social justice perspective that Simpson (2004) calls for in gap year models, volunteers expressed a growing concern for the well-being of others around the world after their year. Their narratives suggest that developing deep relationships with local people during the year helped to provide continued motivation to work to alleviate poverty after their return home. This resonates with Nel Noddings' (1984, 14) argument that moral education involves building relationships through a deep exploration of otherness:

> When we see the other's reality as a possibility for us, we must act to eliminate
> the intolerable, to reduce the pain, to fill the need, to actualize the dream. When
> I am in this sort of relationship with another, when the other's reality becomes a
> real possibility for me, I care.

Stemming from these relationships, some volunteers had "guilt" about the opportunities that they have in their life compared with their friends in their gap year communities, which contributed to their motivations to work for poverty alleviation and concern with the poor in the developing world. These findings overlap with previous studies in intercultural learning (Evans et al. 1987; Kiely 2004), which found that exposing the nonpoor to poverty can lead to changing their sense of cultural allegiance to one of global solidarity with the poor. It also supports previous research that illustrates Mestiza Hart's (2001, 168) contention that, as learners cross contextual borders of race, gender, and class, they develop greater critical awareness of unequal relations of power—what she labeled "mestiza consciousness." Tom, a volunteer in this study, highlighted this when he said he realized after his year: "I'm a white man from England; if I can't make it—than I am rubbish—many people there don't have these opportunities."

Some have proposed that modern, postindustrial society is not well-suited to nurturing these same notions of community life. For example, Alasdair MacIntyre (1981) argues that our common life in the post-Enlightenment West has become too individualistic to adequately transmit and promote virtues. Seen in this light, sending young people to places with a different orientation to material goods and more intimate conception of community may amount to a means of "outsourcing" some of this development of young people—sending them to places, and situating them in social roles, that are more conducive to promoting particular virtues than is the life they might lead at home. Viewing the gap year in these terms highlights its pedagogical and social value but should also lead us to question what it is about life in developed countries that young people sometimes have to leave in order to develop virtues and dispositions that help enrich their personal and public lives.

5

Changes in Ways of Thinking and Future Plans

> I feel like I have matured more in the last year, than I have in the whole 19 years of my life. By seeing, feeling and dealing with situations in the world that I would never have seen myself in, I feel that I have really developed my way of thinking.
> —*Anala*, Peru

> I feel like I learned more in a year than in all of my school education.
> —*Susan*, Honduras

Expanded Worlds

In earlier chapters we looked at how volunteers' experiences with difference in gender roles, morality, and other cultural matters often prompted them to question their own culture, their basic assumptions, and their ways of being. For instance, one volunteer in China reported being pushed to reexamine some of her core beliefs: "I never thought about it before, how we view knowledge and education—it was only when I saw a different way that I thought about it." Likewise, exposure to difference challenged Mark, a volunteer in Honduras, to think about new issues:

> On a deeper level I learned a lot of lessons and things that I had never thought about before because I used to take life in the West for granted. The year helped me start to question further things I had only begun to think about before I went away.

Together, volunteers' narratives suggest that these experiences led them to develop more expanded conceptions about the world, visions more informed by the world's complexity and diversity. One volunteer in Thailand said: "I am humbled by the magnitude, the size of the world. I realized that not everything revolves around me; I don't know everything." Susan, a volunteer teacher in a rural village in Honduras, echoed this expansion of her world and the resulting excitement: "I lived in a bubble of friends and people my age—school, work, friends—that was my world before. Now I realize that there is more to life than me and people my age—and it's exciting to see the world—something outside my little suburban home."

In addition, volunteers suggest that these experiences exposed them—and made them more open—to other worldviews. A volunteer in Guyana expressed this after a year of working with Muslim students:

> The media in the UK views Islam from a more Christian perspective and often portrays Islam as violent. But over my year I saw that it's not; and I thought, if my ideas about Islam are wrong, what else could be? My year opened my mind to criticism and alternative ideas. I was set in my ways before, from Scotland. I've changed my mind; I am more open-minded.

Likewise, Rosie's volunteering in India opened her up to difference:

> My knowledge of the world has been enhanced and my mind has been opened to everything there is that is different from what I thought I knew. The world is a massive, complex, chaotic place, and there are so many fascinating things about it that so many people don't know about. India has inspired me to want to travel everywhere because having an understanding of a culture so different from my own lets me see that life at home is only the tiniest part of what the world is about. I feel I have a far stronger sense of the world and how different it can be from what's immediately on my doorstep.

Chris, a volunteer in Namibia, also felt that the way he understood the world was disrupted, leaving him more aware of his ignorance:

> No matter how much you think you know about the world, going to a place like Lano for a while will make you realize how little you actually knew. I thought I was pretty wise about the ways of the world before I went, but really I knew barely anything—newspapers just don't tell you how it really is.

Reflecting this more "expanded" and "open" orientation to the world, participants also reported a reduction in cultural stereotypes and prejudices. Sam, a volunteer in Japan, recalled how living with and meeting others from around the world helped him to realize that his "stereotypes about certain countries . . . were pretty much wrong." Another volunteer in Japan shared how his year gave him experiences so that he will rethink his stereotypes and be more "fair" in his perspectives of other countries:

Seeing how another country does things reminded me that just because it's not the way I know it doesn't mean it's not a better way. . . It has helped me gain a more fair perspective on which to base my opinions about Asian countries and many other countries around the world.

But it was not just the contrasts that were enlightening. Joanna, a teacher in Uganda, was impressed by the similarities: "My view of the world, and Africa especially, was very tainted by relief organization advertisements; which make Africa seem like another planet. Coming here I've realized that we are all so incredibly similar no matter where we come from. I think I have lost many of the prejudices I held before I came here."

Understanding of Their Home Country

It was not only self-understanding that improved; living elsewhere also shed light on their home country in particular and on the West in general.

For example, Amy, a volunteer who had returned from India, shared: "When you know another culture, it humbles your own culture. It shows you that Western culture is not the be all and end all and that in many ways it is flawed." Similarly, another volunteer said: "I didn't see British culture before, but now I can. Having returned, I am much more aware of the social norms of Scottish society, such as not really paying much attention to other people." A volunteer in Cambodia stated, "I have a different look on my life in England which, surprisingly enough, I didn't expect." Rosie, a volunteer quoted in the section above, elucidated how her experiences in India changed her view of the United Kingdom:

> My outlook on the UK has changed from it being the normal place I call home to being this super organized, safe country where everything works; where there are so many rules and regulations, and people you can turn to for advice; where the government and police are not corrupt; and where everything you expect to happen happens. I left home thinking this was the way the world worked and came back realizing how unique the UK is to have such system.

What triggered this cultural reassessment? One volunteer said that "as you learn about local culture you compare it to the UK and see differences, and people ask questions about the UK culture and life, and you see the differences." Many volunteers felt that there was no substitute, in this respect, to time abroad.

As one said: "I don't think you can properly understand where you come from if you haven't seen other cultures." For a volunteer in the Dominican Republic, only engaging another culture can supply the questions to ask about one's own:

> Until you go overseas I think one's imagination has a huge part in how one envisages things in the world . . . living there allowed their customs to seep into my way of living. I only really understood how much my outlook had changed when I came home; I found myself looking at everything like an outsider, questioning and philosophizing the same way as when I had first arrived in the Dominican Republic. Perhaps what I am trying to say is that questioning the way we live is only possible when you know what you want to ask, and that really can only come when you have seen a comparable way of living.

Relative Nature of the World

But just *how* did volunteers' vision of the world change? For many, as I discuss in this section, the world became more "relative." As one volunteer put it, they came to see that "normal" cultural practices at home were not always "normal" in other cultures.

The key to this particular change, according to volunteers, was integrating into the new culture and thus coming to understand more deeply a different way of being. Take it from Nate, a volunteer teacher in an aboriginal village in the rain forest of Guyana:

> I changed because I lived as a local. I lived as a villager so I was able to see the world from that perspective. I can now see the world and life's arrangements as social constructs, like go to school, go to university, live this way—but it's not necessary—absolutely not. Before I thought that our way of living in the UK was the only way—I wasn't aware of other ways of living. I thought being a lawyer was an important job to have, but it is just not relevant. Like if I become a lawyer it just won't be relevant; being a lawyer is only important in the relevant context. Back in the UK, it's not really relevant. Life in the village was much more relevant—more simple. Your life and your work are directly related to daily life. It makes much more sense—that way of life.

Nate felt adamant that his long-term placement in the village was critical to his changes and newly developed view of the world: "In the short term you don't get that perspective; people are always helping you, like by the end we caught our own fish and set up our own camp—I could have found a wife and lived there—I was at that level." On rare occasions, volunteers did in fact stay in the gap year country and marry a local person.

The effects of such integration run deep. Duncan felt that coming to view the world from (in his case) a "Thai perspective" sparked other changes that have been explored in this book, such as tolerance:

> I feel I am now more independent, more confident, and more knowledgeable about the world. Being part of another culture which is so vastly different from your own opens your eyes to a world that would otherwise be unknown to you. Things which we take as "normal" are merely biased to the culture we grew up in, making everything else seem strange and new. . . . Seeing these places from a Thai perspective (as opposed to the tourist routes that would normally have to be taken) was incredible . . . I think my outlook on the world is broader and I can see that things that we see as unusual are merely just culturally localized to another area of the world. I think I am more tolerant in that I can appreciate differences in the way people do things, knowing that this is just the cultural norm for them.

Gregory, a volunteer in China, also felt that his time abroad increased his tolerance:

> I think before I came here, my preconception of China was that it was as foreign as you can get from Britain, in every way. In fact, the gaps are a lot narrower in many ways, mostly because when we look at the world as children we forget that all these exotic countries are still inhabited by humans, and that's an awful lot to have in common to begin with.

This relativism and ability to place one's home culture and way of being in context was also cultivated in more subtle ways as volunteers adjusted, say, by learning how different cultures communicate. For example, a volunteer in Mauritius said: "I thought it was rude at first, but I learned how to shout to get attention from a shopkeeper . . . I had to yell . . . I realized that the way we communicate in the West is not the way everyone else does." A volunteer in Uganda reports that her experiences with Ugandan dance contributed to her relative understanding of the world: "I realized that it's only because we are white and interpret it as sexual—but it's not . . . dance does not have to be sexual." Volunteers come to appreciate differences in beliefs, not just practices. Daniel, a volunteer in South Africa, said: "If you tell the local people there you do not believe in God, it is not comprehensible to them—and that helps to see your own thinking and values. You realize that their thinking is as natural to them as yours is to you."

Connection to the World and Affiliation with the Home Country

At the same time that volunteers' "worlds" expanded and their views of their home country changed, many also felt more connected to their gap year country and to the world in general. One volunteer in Peru shared: "I feel more connected to the world because I have seen the world, and I care more about the world. I understand issues people are going through more, especially in South America." Another said: "I feel part of the world more . . . because more of the world is my home."

Other volunteers felt more "connected to humanity" or to "people around the world." Samantha, a volunteer in Mauritania, explains: "I think now that no matter how different you think you are from somebody—whether that's to do with religion, nationality, or however—you can always find a common link and be surprised by the similarities you find no matter where you're from." Another echoed this, "I've realized that things don't necessarily change, even if you move thousands of miles across the world—people across the world experience the same problems and difficulties in their lives."

Building relationships and directly witnessing others' lives personalized developing countries for volunteers and heightened their awareness of international affairs. Leah highlighted this: "You personalize the third world; you have relationships with people there and you can understand the issues so much more, and you realize that they are not that different from me." Volunteers also remarked that the ease and speed of travel—especially to places that once seemed incredibly distant—helped them to feel that the world was smaller and more connected.

Sometimes former volunteers indicated that their experiences had modified their sense of their national identity. Some volunteers said they felt "more British" or more "patriotic" after their years. One volunteer said: "I developed a patriotic appreciation of the UK overseas." Many volunteers reported that they "felt British for the first time" over their year, especially as they were seen as an "ambassador" or "representative" of the United Kingdom (or another culture generally) in their gap year community. This sense tended to influence volunteers' behavior; as Sarah explained: "I did not want people to think badly of me and therefore all the UK."

At the same time, many volunteers said they felt less British after their year, as Tim shared: "I feel like I am less British now and more international." Volunteers often developed a strong affiliation and identification with their volunteer country. One said, "I feel part Namibian now," while another shared, "I feel more South African than British now." High levels of immersion seemed to influence this connection to a gap year country; a volunteer from South Africa said: "I left part of my heart there—I was living there as a South African." In another example, a volunteer in Botswana said he feels part Botswanan, part Scottish after his year, and that "the villagers, they called me the white Botswanan. I was so integrated." High levels of local patriotism also seemed to influence this, as one South African volunteer said: "I don't even know the British national anthem, but I know the South African one. The people there are so patriotic; I wish the UK was more like that."

Reassessment of Opportunities

With a greater understanding of life outside of their home in Europe—and the inequalities that exist between developed and developing nations—many volunteers said they had become more grateful for their lives, opportunities, and home country. John, a volunteer in Botswana, felt "humbled" by a new awareness of his opportunities: "I have gained a greater appreciation of my parents and friends and I have a greater understanding of my own abilities and limits as well. The whole year has humbled me, and I realize now actually how much I have at home and I am extremely grateful for that."

This increase in appreciation was often triggered by going without—without things like one's family, public policy provisions, or a culturally familiar environment—and recognizing what those missing factors provide. Gregory, a volunteer in China, highlighted this:

> I'm more aware of the fact that the majority of the world is poor and has extremely limited financial freedom, which in turn makes me appreciate how much I have. Growing up in the UK, I remember the inevitable comparisons made between other classmates: "I wish I had a car like that; I wish I could go to Mexico; I want a coat like that, saying Rockport, etc." Everything is relative and now that I have something different to relate my life to, I can see how good a deal we all have just for being British and European.

Megan, a volunteer in China, said two years after her experiences abroad that her motivation and appreciation of opportunities came from the children she was teaching and her sense of "guilt:"

My gap year gave me a drive to make something of myself. I have motivations to do things, to not waste time, to make use of my time—you can be quite lazy as a teenager. In China, the kids worked so hard—they work so hard for absolutely nothing. I have opportunities that they will never have, and I feel guilty for not taking all of them—like I am a spoiled child.

Likewise, after Faye returned home from South Africa, she knew she had changed: "I am no longer content in doing nothing. Since I have returned I feel like I should be doing more 'good' things with my life, like filling the hours I would have usually been watching TV with doing something better—like trying to do some more voluntary work."

Many volunteers also grew in their appreciation of their own education, their previous teachers, and the challenges of being a teacher, especially after having been a teacher themselves. In fact, some volunteers even sent messages or went back to their school to thank—and sometimes apologize to—their teachers, as this one did: "When I was in India, I sent emails to my teachers back in Scotland to thank my teachers and apologize for being arrogant and for not turning up to class and speaking out." In addition, volunteers often reported an increased appreciation of education in the West, especially the British education system and its focus on critical thinking rather than the memorization often found in developing countries. One volunteer said after experiencing an education system riddled with problems, "I appreciate what my teachers did for me; I see now that they were really good teachers."

On top of this, recognizing the relative nature of culture and experiencing new ways of being, returned volunteers often became more aware of the *choice* they have about what sort of life to live, what things to value. Betty, a volunteer in Peru, typified this view of seeing life as a privilege and a choice:

My outlook on the world has changed a great deal since being in Peru. I now regard my future, going to university and starting a career, as a huge privilege—because I have the choice to study and choose what I want to do in life. What is so difficult to accept is that a lot of the children in the Aldea will not have that choice.

Volunteers saw education in particular as a privilege, which increased their motivation in college. Jordan highlighted this common sentiment: "I am really critical of people who come straight from school now, who go out every night and don't care about their degree because they just want to get a degree and get money afterwards. I think education is a privilege now, especially at this level, but I didn't think that before; without my gap year I probably would have been one of those people."

Future Volunteering

Many people also felt that their gap year had influenced their perspectives and intentions about volunteering. Many said that they were more motivated to volunteer and do charitable work by their experiences with poverty, deeper ability to empathize, new appreciation of community life, and increased self-efficacy. Matt, a teacher in a rural village in Guyana, said: "Before my year I used to think about what I can get from society, but now I think about what I can give to society." Another gap year participant said: "I want to do charitable work; I want to make changes and improve the lives of others, but on the grassroots level and in other sectors."

Laura, a volunteer in Chile, said she now understood poverty on a more personal level:

> After this year, I now feel a lot closer to the poverty we see on television. Although I always knew it was not just an image, they suddenly become a lot more of a reality to me when I saw it with my own eyes and have known people from such backgrounds. I have got to know places that I would have never visited on a holiday and through this I have met many people who are very special and unique in their ways of life. I am much more enthusiastic about helping others in need and a lot more understanding towards their situations and difficulties.

For Leah, a year in Namibia "personalized the third world." She explained: "You have friends there and you have relationships there, so it strikes you in a real way when you see it on the news. You lived amongst that . . . I want to work more for poverty; I want to raise awareness and inspire others." Another volunteer said that after his year he "can see a greater link" between the poor in the United Kingdom and himself, and as a result he said he is "more likely to help in UK."

Sometimes a growing recognition of "injustice" or a feeling of "social responsibility" provided the motivation to volunteer. Kara, a volunteer in Chile, said that over the year: "I learned about the injustice in society; people should learn more how to share in life, by giving and gaining." Becky, who was in South Africa, said: "I think I feel more socially responsible, which I think is why I'm keen to keep volunteering in the future. Politically I think I've had a sense of responsibility for quite a few years, but I think my year reinforced the importance of that, especially on international issues."

For Susan, a volunteer in Honduras, it was an increased self-efficacy and sense of community that made her feel more able and motivated to help others:

> I am more aware of the importance of community, and now that I'm back I see
> my home place as a community and I am much more likely to get involved in
> kids' groups; scouts. There are so many things you can get involved with. I want
> to do more volunteering in my community; I know I have the skills now. Before
> gap year I thought what do I have to offer? Why would they want the help of just
> some kid? But now I realize I can help and I have something to offer. I want to
> visit elderly people in hospital, work with underprivileged groups; organize trips
> with university groups and get involved in campaigns and charities and some
> overseas. . . . Before I only volunteered for my resume; now I do it just because
> I want to, the satisfaction from it, from seeing others happy and helping others,
> knowing how much people need companionship or role models—like young
> kids—I can be that. . . . Now there is just so much more to life.

People frequently acted upon these increased desires to volunteer during college. Many reported continuing to fundraise for their gap year causes, raise awareness, and volunteer again in their gap year countries or elsewhere overseas.

Understanding New Issues and Forming Opinions

Volunteers said they were better able to understand issues in the world after their year abroad. More specifically, they said that having a greater range of personal experiences gives them more points of reference and comparisons in making meaning and in placing situations in cultural contexts. One volunteer explained how this occurs for him: "I now relate new things and issues to a wider range of personal experiences, like when you see things on the media or things in life, you have a bank of ideas to help understand them. It is nice to think about things in different perspectives, and satisfying to make those connections." Another volunteer described a similar experience:

> I also gained a huge amount of life experience, living and working in a commu-
> nity and culture totally different from that in Scotland, and I learnt so much
> from people a lot younger than me. I think I have gained a unique outlook on life
> because I have taken the many experiences I had, the work that I did, the people

I met and also the things that I saw whilst in Peru and have applied them to the way I see my life here in Scotland.

Similarly, Robert observed that, when trying to understand another culture, he learned to look for more cultural nuances and "differences beneath the sur-face." Volunteers also reported becoming more aware of cultural differences after living in another culture. Matt, a volunteer in Guyana, said: "I am much more culturally sensitive and aware here in the UK, and I am more empathetic with immigrants and other cultures."

Often, volunteers believed that they are better able to understand social problems after their gap year. One said: "I think now I'm much more aware of things going on that before I had no idea about and the social problems societies other than my own face." Echoing this, Laura said: "I have returned from Chile more socially aware and with a greater knowledge and understanding of other cultures. I have definitely grown as a person, in the way I look at the world." Likewise, Samantha felt that she is "more able to understand other countries and their problems."

Volunteers also often felt that they had become more independent and critical in their thinking and perspectives on issues in their lives. One said: "I think I am a much more independent thinker now, able to draw on and evaluate multiple influences before formulating an opinion." Another said: "I have greater per-spective on elements of my life . . . I am less neurotic than my friends . . . I don't sweat the small stuff; I can see the world from many different perspectives."

Applying this critical thinking, many volunteers believed they had developed a more critical stance on the media and cultural messages after encountering biases and inaccuracies during their year. For instance, Leah said that, after her year in Namibia, she is "wary of leaders and media . . . I don't just trust what others say and accept it as truth; I read for myself. I read other things before deciding what the truth is." Florence, a volunteer in South Africa, said: "From this experience, I now have a more rounded outlook on how different cultures and countries work, and I am more critical of the media's judgment of different countries' problems."

This was especially evident among volunteers in China. Volunteers who spent their year there often reported becoming more critical and skeptical about media. One volunteer, after being a teacher in China and experiencing the strong gov-ernment influence in media, said:

My time in China made me question the idea of media and knowledge and truth, and how it is just a perspective. I approach information and knowledge differently now. In China you learn to be skeptical of what is being said; for example, the news, it's not as it appears. I trust the media much less now . . . also there is lots of freedom there—which is not what I expected or is portrayed in the West. I learned that there are different sides of every story.

Volunteers also grew more critical of Western media. One volunteer said: "Our media is so negative about China. For example, the minority started a riot but the media portrayed it as it was by horrible communists. I am more critical of the media now; I can't believe everything I see from it." Another volunteer in China developed criticism of Western media portrayals of cultures in developing countries:

Being amongst the minorities of Xinjiang has taught me about how ignorant the Western world generally is about different cultures in developing countries. I'm now far less inclined now to simply follow sensationalist media and sentiments (e.g., Free Tibet) and more interested in finding out the complete picture behind any one problem.

In addition to developing a critical perspective on information, volunteers often thought that their gap year experiences increased their ability to make decisions, solve problems, and form their own views. Many cited increased overall confidence, clarified personal values, and frequent occasions to make important decisions as factors in these changes. For instance, one former volunteer said: "I feel like I know more about what I want out of life and who I am has become clearer to me, so I've developed in the way that I can make decisions more easily and be stronger in my opinions." Likewise, Joanna said: "I have certainly become more confident. I feel more secure in my own opinions and better able to formulate and develop my own views on issues." Tim, a volunteer in Botswana, said that "now I am more sure about the decisions I make and what I think." Many also felt that they were better able to express their views; a volunteer in Thailand shared this sentiment: "I now feel that I have valid opinions to share; why not?" A woman who volunteered in South Africa shared her newly developed confidence and voice: "I have become a much more open person, and able to speak my mind if I don't believe that something is right."

People who went from being volunteers to being at universities in the United Kingdom often described how the year developed their desires and abilities to understand others' perspectives and the implications of their decisions. Megan, who was in China, said: "I am a better decision-maker now because I have a more rounded approach. . . . Over my year I learned that even though you think there is only one way to do things—others can do it differently. I can see how different things can be done, even if they don't seem to work at first." Abigail said she is now more "careful to understand all sides of a story or issue before making any judgment on it," citing her work with children in Malawi as a major influence. John, a volunteer in Botswana, said: "My actions are more mature and premeditated," while Dominic said: "I am more able to think through the consequences of my decisions." As one volunteer succinctly put it: "I think about others more when I make decisions."

A Greater Desire to Learn and Travel

This growing sense of the enormity and diversity of the world—combined with the experience of living overseas and learning about new cultures—seemed to ignite a strong interest in traveling and learning more about the world in almost all the volunteers. People often felt "awakened" and more "motivated," as well as more "appreciative" of educational opportunities, as discussed above. One said: "My interests broadened; they are new and different; I care about more things, like campaigns . . . I really had my eyes opened to the world; I am more interested in other cultures and countries. There is so much more out there to see, enjoy, and experience."

Likewise, a volunteer in India reported after returning from her gap year: "It feels unsatisfactory to not know about where you are. When I got back to Scotland, I was asking why people act this way, why is it different from England? How is it the same; I just wanted to know more." Another volunteer illustrated his changing orientation to the unknown in the world: "I have also learned not to be afraid of new and foreign places—or people. Although they live in a completely different community, people are still people and I realized that in today's day and age it is important to understand, experience and question why certain communities run the way they do and why people live in the conditions they live in."

Leah, a volunteer in Namibia, thought her year piqued her "curiosity to find out about the world. I was awakened more—to find out different stances—positions—to understand the world. Since coming back, I am a lot more curious." After her gap year "burst [her] suburban bubble," Susan, a volunteer in Honduras, said: "I feel like I learned more in a year than in all my school education. I'm rejuvenated about education and want to go back to university."

Furthermore, volunteers often said they were more "ambitious" or wanted to "get more from life" after their gap year. For instance, Kyle, a volunteer in Guyana, said that he was now "more excited for life in general and desire to take advantage of opportunities and be part of life's affairs." Jess, a volunteer in India, shared how her gap year and its challenge and accomplishments changed her motivation: "The year also helped me to learn how to make the most of situations. It didn't last long so I had to enjoy every minute or at least make the most out of everything and I want to apply that way of living to the rest of my life. It was amazing the things I managed to achieve in that year and I want to continue life, achieving and challenging myself."

In contrast to their secondary school and lives before, some volunteers believed the gap year was a helpful break and allowed greater opportunities to explore new areas of interest. One said:

> I really didn't enjoy high school. . . . I had no time to read or explore issues or topics that I wanted to explore, but over the gap year I had quite a lot of time—to read into topics and subjects. For my community report, because I wrote on something I was interested in—Japan. It was the longest but most enjoyable piece of writing ever in my life. I really want to learn now, more about culture, more about the world, more about everything.

Others said the gap year provided opportunities and "time to read" that they did not have before in their "busy" or "cluttered" lives. One person, who volunteered in a library to help children during her gap year shared: "Before my year I didn't read books, but I started reading over the year, and now I read a lot."

Exposure to new experiences widened volunteers' range of interests. Tobias, a volunteer we met in the previous chapter who wanted to use his gap year to become more extroverted, said that computer games had been a "big part" of his adolescence. He said: "I played 1,000 hours a year. I came home from school and played World of Warcraft; that was it." However, despite playing the game early in his year abroad, he grew to think that "computer games are a waste of time—they are an easy way out of doing anything, like a drug to put things out of your mind. There is so much you could actually do and learn outside." Another volunteer said: "Before I used to say I was bored. I never say that anymore; there is so much to do or I can find things to do."

Taking a gap year also sparked an interest in international affairs, especially as volunteers felt more "connected to the world" and their gap year country and developed relationships with the people in these countries. Volunteers felt they could personalize the developing world and a greater range of news stories. Further, many also felt that—ever since they were part of their gap year country's affairs and have "invested" in the country, working toward its improvement—they continue to follow its affairs. One volunteer said: "I definitely care more about politics and international affairs now. . . . I watch the news more, especially about Latin America."

Two China volunteers said: "I watch the news about China more than about the UK" and "I am much more interested in politics now." Another said: "My year has definitely increased my interest in international politics and in the way China perceives and copes with the Western world—a subject I'd be more than happy to expand on in my university study." Some volunteers reported that their interests were expanded by living in communities where politics were especially prevalent. Noah was one example: "I never really paid attention to politics much before, but we were immersed in politics in Namibia—it only gained independence 20 years ago, and I saw how important politics can be."

A Change in Plans

Many volunteers reported that their gap year experiences altered their immediate or college plans, as they reimagined their role in the world. Although it is rare, some volunteers do not immediately return to their home countries, instead staying to work, continue a romantic relationship with a local person, or even to attend college in the gap year country. Volunteers also sometimes return to their gap year countries to continue working with their projects; in one case a volunteer was still working for the same organization three years after her gap year ended.

Most of the volunteers who decided against college upon returning were already hesitant about going to college before their year. For instance, one volunteer stated:

> Now I don't know if I want to commit for 3 years to something, to university. You're locked down—I had the best time of my life on my year and university would seem boring and not as great. I want to travel more and do another year abroad, plus after my year I worked for two months in South Africa running a camp, and I saw that I could get a good job and that people will hire me without a university degree. I don't need to go to university.

It is also significant that this volunteer developed a romantic relationship with a South African man while overseas and wanted to find more time to spend with him. She added that because she is now more aware of the world and feels she can make it without college, for her "it may have been easier to go straight to university without a gap year," but she certainly "did not regret" taking her year. Another volunteer reported changing his views about college: "I see less value in a university degree because I saw that you can get by and have a good life without one. I'm not going to university; I realized that I didn't need it."

Sometimes, volunteers decided to take another gap year. Susan, a volunteer in Uganda, was planning to enter the Royal Air Force, not college, after her initial gap year. Instead, she ended up taking a second gap year in India. She realized:

> I want to live overseas—I want to do international development, be overseas, and feel like I am helping someone. I don't want to feel like I am behind a desk . . . There are lots of things in development—I only have experience in teaching, and that is not going to help me really. I am going to try to get more work experience for aid organizations—but not go to university—it is detached from the real world. I need "on the ground experience" in international development work.

Some volunteers who did not plan on attending college before starting their gap year continued on their career plans as they had before. For instance, Dan, a volunteer in Uganda, headed for the navy after his gap year as planned, while another volunteer headed back to work on his family's farm in Scotland after his year in Botswana.

Heading to College

Most volunteers returned to Europe and attended a university, often reporting being "more excited" for college after their gap year. One said: "This kind of gap year can be really empowering . . . if I can do a gap year, then I can do university." Many volunteers said they wanted to accomplish more after their gap year, as this volunteer said: "I am more ambitious; I want to do things and accomplish more in life."

Many volunteers reported that having a break from formal education was helpful for their educational careers and contributed to this enthusiasm. For instance, a volunteer in China said: "I am excited about learning new things at university. I am not sick of studying anymore. I have taken a break." Another volunteer said: "The gap year was a really good break from the routine I got stuck in in school. . . . I needed to do something completely different to get out of the routine I was in. Going away changed my attitude toward school, university, and academics. I am willing to sit down and study." Paul said: "I am more prepared to learn. I had a break; now I'm ready." Beth shared this feeling of being more excited and prepared to learn: "I have got back my 'get up and go' which I lost during sixth form [twelfth grade], becoming bored and really rather lazy. I'm excited to go to university and study." Tim, a volunteer in South Africa, reported: "The transition to university was easier; entering a new environment seemed less of a challenge since I had done it before. You know what it is going to involve."

For some volunteers, the gap year seemed to help create a mental and physical distance from school that allowed greater independence of thought about their future. Volunteers reported having "space to think" or "time to think" over their year. John, a volunteer in Botswana, said that "having had time to think about what I want to do with my life has led me to alter my course at university." Mark, a volunteer in Honduras, said that "I learnt to relax and question what I actually want from life, instead of doing things for other people all the time. The problem is I am more confused than when I went!"

As illustrated in earlier chapters, many volunteers described feeling that the decision to go to college was now their "choice," something they were *deciding* to do, rather than part of society's trajectory for them, the next step along the "academic treadmill." For instance, one volunteer shared: "It is a choice to go back to education, to university. I now have a better attitude; I am more focused, and I want to learn."

Some participants reported that their experiences changed their behavior in their years at college, and they did not go out drinking alcohol and partying nearly as often as the other students, especially in the first year. One said: "I feel like I don't need to have a lot of fun in university—because I had that in a year away." A volunteer in China, who said he did drink alcohol in China, said: "I feel more mature than first year students. I won't drink my first year away like I would have done without my gap year. I see other things in life to do that are more important than wasting away drinking." Another former volunteer said she does not drink in college very much after realizing with her gap year partner that "we do not have to drink to have fun."

Coming back from their year, many volunteers also said they wanted, as one put it, "to get more out of university." Participants reported that they were more likely to join clubs, societies, and sports at college. John, a volunteer in Japan, explained: "I think my experience at university will be much more varied and interesting. After having had so many opportunities in my gap year, I intend to make as much of everything that university has to offer, something I might have previously said but not done otherwise." Volunteers frequently cited an increased desire to challenge themselves and to continue to learn from new experiences. Indeed, many were quite involved in clubs and societies in college, and they felt that their greater involvement was due to their gap year. People also reported staying in touch with friends from their gap year country and socializing with fellow gap year volunteers and immigrants from the country at college, advocacy, and fundraising work.

As seen in chapters 2 and 3, many volunteers reported becoming more confident in social settings and feeling better able to express themselves. When they entered college, gap year participants said they participated more in their classes and in their departments. One said, "Because of my year I am more able to participate in class or give a paper and just not worry about it as much." Others felt they were overall "better students" because of their time away, new perspectives, and greater motivation to learn. Economic researchers from Australia and the UK on students who took a gap year supports this idea. They found a significant positive impact on students' academic performance in college, with the strongest impact for students who had applied to college with grades on the lower end of the distribution.

Studies and Jobs after College

Volunteers' often reported that their vocational trajectory—both what type of job they sought and the intensity of their search—was affected by their gap year experiences—but not uniformly. To begin, some participants were reaffirmed in their original college major. Zoe, a volunteer in Chile, said: "It has made me want to go to university and study geography even more." Samantha, a volunteer in an orphanage in South Africa, reported, "My experience overseas has reassured me that my place at university is the right thing to do when I arrive back home. I want to learn more about childhood development. . . . I know I want to pursue a career with children in some way." However, some volunteers left the gap year not knowing what they wanted to do. A volunteer in Namibia said: "In the long run it may help me decide what my future career is, but I am saying no more, I am still very undecided but I now have an inkling of what I may want to do."

That said, Project Trust, a leading gap year provider, estimates that about 50 percent of its volunteers change their major at college after their gap year, either adding an area of study or completely changing it to reflect a new interest such as teaching or international affairs. Volunteers' desires and abilities to change were often mitigated by the ease of doing so and the degree's availability.

Often, these changes reflect new interests or values cultivated during the gap year, such as a change to international relations or to social work. Henry, who changed from history to biomedical sciences and Chinese, said that in making his college decision before his gap year, "I just picked something I was naturally good at—rather than my interests." Volunteers often felt pressured to select their course of study before their gap year what they saw as too early in their lives, as well as to select paths that seemed important in society and had social prestige, like law. Demonstrating this, one volunteer said that, while before his gap year he thought law was important and that he wanted to work in a "big firm in London," he realized that these arrangements are just "social constructs" and his law trajectory in London was "not relevant" to much of the world. Further, volunteers often reported that having time to reflect and think outside of their home society about what they wanted to do was important in modifying their vocational track.

Sometimes, volunteers cited specific experiences over their year as motivating their vocational change. For example, Jamie said that her experiences as a teacher overseas motivated her to switch from chemistry to primary education in college. Similarly, one volunteer said, "I never considered teaching before, but I loved teaching students—it is a definite career option now." A volunteer who worked with street youth over her year said: "My gap year has made me think that to work in the child care field, especially with troubled youth, could be an option for my career. Although it can be extremely tough at times, it can also be the most rewarding and satisfying job." Sometimes, a volunteer's secondary project overseas inspired a new vocational path. Leah, a volunteer in Namibia, started and ran an outreach and Bible study group for young girls. She said: "This is what I want to do in a career."

Other volunteers learned that they did *not* want to extend their gap year professional role into a career. One, who was registered for a degree in education in college before his year, said: "As for the long-term future, I know that teaching is not in store for me. I feel the year I spent teaching is enough to carry me through life and it has steered me clear of that profession!" Another volunteer said that after his year of teaching, he "realized that I just do not have the patience to be a teacher."

In addition, in changing their majors, many volunteers often selected courses and desired vocational paths that would allow them to continue learning about and be involved with cultures and places around the world. A volunteer who had spent his year in Thailand changed his college so he could study Thai and religion. A volunteer in India illustrated her decision in changing her major:

My experience has affected what I'm studying at university. I had wanted to be a lawyer, but the more time I spent away from living a Western life, the less I wanted to have a secure job worthy degree. I changed my mind because I wanted to expand my knowledge of the world and travel into less developed countries to get to know other fascinating cultures. I've realized over this year that there really is so much more to learn and there is so much out there that we just don't think about in our day to day lives. I wanted to be involved in the bigger picture, or at least to have an understanding of it, and I wanted a degree that would allow me to go off on more adventures like the one I had on my year in India, so I'm now studying politics and international relations.

Many of the volunteers in China changed their course of study. Mary said: "I want to speak Chinese and learn more about it . . . I changed my degree to Chinese and politics—now I want to do diplomacy, work in the civic service, on the fast track program." In fact, in one cohort of gap year students I studied for this book, a majority of volunteers in China changed their major to Chinese or added courses on China to their undergraduate education.

Many participants indicated that they were looking for a more general emphasis on careers that allow them to engage with and help others after their gap year. For one, "being in Cambodia gave me the opportunity to realize I definitely want to work to benefit others. As a result of this I have decided to study social sciences instead of English language." Another volunteer changed her degree to reflect her desire to serve others: "I was going to do history before, but that seemed superfluous, and I changed to nursing. I care more about the suffering of others and alleviating it now. History seemed like a pointless exercise given my gap year experiences, so I changed my course to reflect my new priorities; I have greater opportunities to use my skills there." Others were moved less by disenchantment with one path than attraction to another: "My aspiration before was a boring office job; now want to do something that will make me happy and fulfilled, like teaching; there is so much pleasure in helping children." Another volunteer put it succinctly: "I care less about money in my career and more about fulfillment." Kara reported that her year in Chile changed the way she thinks one should focus one's energies in the world: "I realized I want to use my talents to improve other people's quality of life . . . and to give them a different prospective on life. I want to let people feel hope, prosperity and self-confident of their own talents."

Often, volunteers who did not change their overall course of study did plan (as a result of their gap year) to use their degree in more international or more charitable domains. For instance, medical students often said they wanted to serve in Médecins Sans Frontières (Doctors Without Borders), focus on public health, or practice overseas after finishing school. One medical student who had been a volunteer said: "I now want to practice overseas for a bit . . . for a few years in a developing country." Abigail shared: "Just as I planned before India I started studying biomedical sciences, but I just really know now what I want to do with it, and I'm trying to become a basic doctor besides just a researcher, because that would be really useful in developing countries." Or another volunteer, Marsha, who reported, "Now I can't wait to do internships or research abroad. To come back to countries like India with more skills and try to make myself useful. I honestly can't wait to get my degree and do medical research and work in developing countries."

After changing their studies to fit their new interests, many volunteers said they were more interested in their major and often used their experiences during their gap year to reflect and supplement material provided in class. This was true of those studying the language or culture of their gap year country or fields related to their experiences. For example, a volunteer studying international development observed that his time in Uganda has helped "ground" the theory he is learning in college. One participant said after switching from her degree in art, "I switched because I love the language, so now I put so much more into it, but I didn't put my heart into art before."

Even though many volunteers did not change their major, they often altered the focus or courses that make up their degree. Robert thought that his work in Mauritania shaped his academic focus: "I lean towards African history wherever possible in my history degree at college because I now have that connection with the continent and a genuine interest in how it became the way it is today." Another volunteer reported after her year, "I still want to go to university and study biology although through my years at university I am now considering concentrating on the anthropology side of the subject." In addition, many volunteers conduct research or write their senior theses on subjects related to their gap year country. Jen, who was a teacher in Chile, did her senior thesis on education policy in Chile, while another student did hers on language in Guyana.

Sometimes volunteers developed a desire to live outside of their home country after their year: "When jobs and after university are considered I think that I know that I will not want to live here but somewhere else different." Patricia said: "I have now changed my course at university to include a language, Spanish. This will affect my career a lot and hopefully leave me working in a Spanish speaking country later in life!" In fact, it is not uncommon for former gap year volunteers to live overseas, working in business, international organizations, or government.

Some volunteers, however, remained undecided about what to study after their gap year. Some, like Cara, a volunteer in India, decided to take another year before starting college: "I am taking another year out to decide what to do at university." Another said: "I am still undecided, but my thoughts about careers are more varied and ambitious." On the whole, though, volunteers reported returning with more awareness of a wider range of career options.

Difficulties in Returning Home

As volunteers' perspectives of themselves, the world, and their role in it shifted, some found it difficult to return to their home countries. Even two to three years after returning from their gap year, some volunteers struggled to integrate their gap year experiences with their lives back home. One volunteer described his challenge as "trying to fit a third world perspective into the first world." Another volunteer who spent his year in the rainforest in Guyana described an intense "struggle to contemplate upon [his] year" and that his experience "was so removed from normal life back home that, now that I have returned, the whole year now takes on a very dream-like state."

His struggle was not unique; volunteers frequently reported feeling out of place or even guilty about leaving the volunteering project. One volunteer felt she "left her heart in South Africa with the kids" she was working with. Some described a feeling that their newfound potential to contribute is not being reached in college, but many volunteers tried to "keep their gap year alive" and stay involved in their gap year project, through news, friendships, donations, research, awareness, or trips back to the community even years afterward. Nevertheless, many volunteers said they were able to overcome many challenges of readjustment in their first year of college, developing as "better" students in the long term.

Volunteers often reported "return culture shock" after their gap year that was "harder to deal with" than the initial culture shock they experienced overseas—one even described it as "sickening" to see a place "you thought you knew in a very different light." Volunteers, having come from cultures they perceived were "friendly" and "outgoing," often grew disappointed by the perceived lack of friendliness at home. One recalled that in Botswana he had just left the "happiest culture and nicest people I have ever met," but he "went to passport control—and there was not a happy greeting . . . it was really disappointing." Another volunteer was frustrated at the "British reserve" she encountered while greeting people on the street soon after her return. Some volunteers had difficulty readjusting to British English, weather, and customary greetings; one volunteer said that at a family party she went to go give the "customary" Chilean "double-kiss," and her family member was "startled." Another volunteer was "comparing the UK to Guyana" early in his gap year, but comparing "Guyana to the UK" on his return, which prompted him to question many aspects of life that he had previously taken for granted.

As seen in chapter 2, many returned volunteers reported increased motivation to take advantage of opportunities than they would have before going on their gap year. Many do take them—but some also felt guilty about having so many options when the people they had lived with in their gap year community do not. Megan said that two years after her gap year in China, she still feels the guilt of her newly recognized opportunities:

> You try to be like them, to live like them, but you can always escape; after one year you can come back and you have all these opportunities, but they are there forever—that makes me guilty—I am still the rich foreigner and I won't be in such poverty. You can get really close to them and they'll call you their daughter, but they will never look at me as one of them.

Another volunteer, who worked in an orphanage in South Africa, brought photographs of "her children" in South Africa to our interview, nearly tearing up while talking about them and how she felt so "guilty" for leaving them. Citing this guilt and attachment, many returned volunteers went back to see their projects and "children" during college.

Specifically, having the opportunity to attend higher education in the developed world was challenging for many volunteers upon return. In fact, Amy, a volunteer in India, described her frustration with university life (as "separated" and "quite selfish") and her lack of adjustment to it, saying, "If I couldn't go back this summer to India to the project I would drop out of university." Amy felt that being in college was "like leading a double life, that I have two homes: one here and one in India that sometimes interact. I have my friends here but they don't want to hear it, but then I have my friends in India and we talk and chat." Like other volunteers, Amy expressed frustration with college life: "I feel a little bit pointless here in university; it feels like I am doing nothing. There is really no responsibility in university; although I am learning things I am really interested in, I do question what the use of it is." Amy remarked that she did not have the opportunity to reflect on her year, and she still has not, which she believes contributes to her feelings of dissonance, a concept that is explored further in chapter 6:

> In some ways I didn't really reflect on my year when I was abroad. I was always going and doing and never stopping, and in some ways that lead me to that it was incomplete, and feel that it was unfinished because I haven't had that space to reflect upon it a lot. But I am hoping that will come this summer when I go back to India, that being back there will help me think about it more.

James, a volunteer working with street youth in Bolivia, talked about his experience coming back to the United Kingdom and into his elite university:

> Seeing somewhere where you thought you knew in a whole different light, it is sickening, seeing first world from third world perspective. Everything is straight in first world . . . You come back and you can't handle it, it's like two separate lives. Your brain can't handle it; it is so alien, so you feel as if it didn't happen. You can't fit it in your head. You just have to suppress it, the differences; they are just too large you can't make them fit. Last week I was at my college's 500 year anniversary, and I was wearing coat tails and spent 90 pounds on dinner and I thought what the f**k am I doing? That could have paid for wages for Consuelos for a year.

James also echoed Megan's feeling of the inherent separation between a volunteer and a local community. He, too, was acutely aware of the divides between the developed and developing world, and of their injustice:

> You try to be like common people there, but it is not the same if you have a return ticket; you can press escape button and rewind. This is not fair; how am I allowed to do this and they are not allowed to do this. And it's so unchangeable; they can't get a visa to the UK; they would have to show that they had 30,000 pounds, but I could just fly down; that is the injustice, how massively unjust, how shit the boundary between the third world and first world is. Living here feels like you cheated, that it is not fair to your friends back in Bolivia, that it's not just.

Some volunteers also reported feeling that they had difficulties sympathizing with their peers' problems, which they had come to see as less important in the larger context of the world. Tom, a volunteer in South Africa, exemplified this: "I also find it quite hard to listen to friends moan and complain about how their parents are so annoying and this and that. I just end up thinking about asking them how important they believe their problem is just to see whether they'd give an interesting answer." Or another volunteer: "In the UK, people complain and worry about things that people in other parts of the world just get on with." Shifts in volunteers' views of problems and their interests also contributed to the loss of friendship between volunteers and older friends from their home communities, as seen in the chapter on interpersonal relations.

As volunteers came to appreciate and desire a "less materialistic life" (as discussed in chapter 4), they often had difficulty reentering their home country and facing pressure to buy and consume. Leah, for instance, recalled:

> I came back and went to a store in Oban, and it just overwhelmed me; I felt all this outside pressure to buy . . . these desires to buy and feed ourselves—this is horrible—we need to get out. I packed only one bag for my gap year and got on fine for a year—my year was so much more important than what I was wearing. After I left the store, I challenged myself to think why am I dependent . . . why did that fear overwhelm me at the store.

Gender roles were another topic on which returned volunteers' changed perspective caused tension. Dan, a volunteer in Guyana said: "I came home and I was pissed at my dad and brother for not helping around the house—in Guyana men in my area helped." Likewise, volunteers also clashed with their parents when they came back home because they felt a greater independence, as we saw in chapter 3.

Many volunteers also often described a changing sense of time and their own productivity after their year. Time was often framed as a space to "accomplish" tasks; volunteers often felt that they "could always be doing more" or were often "wasting time." As one volunteer put it, "It is the problem of potentiality—after you know your potential and see what you can do, you never really feel like you are reaching that point when you are back." Feeling that one could be contributing more to the world, returned volunteers in college, like Amy, cited above, sometimes felt that their home culture was "selfish" or "isolating," or "lacked responsibility." Many volunteers struggled as they felt "selfish" in academic life at college, focusing on themselves and their academic pursuits rather than others.

Compounding some of the challenges of reintegration into their home country, participants often reported feeling unable to share their experiences with peers in higher education, who themselves seemed uninterested. One volunteer found no support in coping with an incident from her gap year: "A student in the school died from an eating disorder there . . . it was really hard coming home. No one understood what I had been through . . . I had an expectation of support from people back home." Some volunteers recognized that, because their peers had not had similar experiences, they were often uninterested in the same topics and could not really empathize with their experiences.

At the same time, volunteers back in college often held back stories of their experiences because of a desire not to seen as a "gap year casualty." This term is used for someone who talks too much about his or her gap year in college and cannot seem to "move on." Many volunteers reported that they feared being labeled or perceived as such and consequently suppressed their impulses to talk about their gap year. James, for instance, discussed the challenge in not sharing his experiences and thoughts about his gap year: "It is such an isolating experience; no one is interested. You can't deal with it; you put it away in a locked box, and people don't want to hear about your experiences either . . . it is really challenging." This suppression of thoughts about the year was widespread and problematic, especially in cases where volunteers felt that something traumatic had happened to them over the year, such as the death of a child in their care or direct experiences with others' suffering.

These traumatic experiences can be very difficult for volunteers to process. As we saw in an earlier chapter, one volunteer who had children in her care die and who put up a "wall" around her emotions to make it through the year, revealed that even after a year, she still "couldn't cry" anymore. Another volunteer, Samantha, discussed her experiences with children in poverty and suffering: "During the year you have to move on when you see it to keep going . . . I never got the chance to deal with it . . . talking about negative things that happened during the year is hard now because I just moved on during the year."

Emphasizing that volunteers can sometimes be pushed too hard or given too much responsibility, a provider staff member reported the challenges facing some returned volunteers, especially those who worked in social care projects. The volunteers in Peru who devoted themselves to the 18 boys in their orphanage needed psychological counseling after separating from the boys when the volunteers returned home. As will be discussed in chapter 8 on designing the gap year, there are worries about exposing young people to certain experiences of suffering, or in situations in which volunteers are overstretched, that need to be considered.

Benefits in College Placements and Hiring

Finally, it seems that, despite some reports of people or institutions dismissing gap years, many volunteers felt that others recognized the value of their experiences. Some reported that having their gap year on their application to college helped them to gain admission. One said: "My grades were not good enough to get in, but they said because I was doing the gap year next year they would let me in." Another volunteer said that her year "helped me getting my place at university."

During and after college, returned volunteers also described having an advantage in applying to jobs—especially, of course, when the gap year experiences had direct relevance. Some older former volunteers thought that their gap year was one of the main reasons that they were hired. One 27-year-old said: "I have never had a job interview where they didn't bring up my gap year and were impressed . . . they thought it was really interesting."

Analysis

This chapter focused on how gap year experiences broadened volunteers' worldviews and affected their ideas about their futures.

These narratives suggest that gap years helped volunteers develop a more relative and contextual way of making sense of the world. As one volunteer said, "Everything is relative now"; another said he saw the world from a "villager's perspective," realizing that our ways of doing things are just "social constructs." Volunteers also became more open to revising their opinions; as a volunteer in Guyana said after his year spent working with Muslim students: "My year opened my mind to criticism and alternative ideas. I was set in my ways before, from Scotland. I've changed my mind; I am more open-minded."

It is also possible that volunteers cultivated a greater "disposition to think critically," which Ernest Pascarella and Patrick Terenzini outline as the inclination to "ask challenging questions and follow the reasons and evidence wherever they lead, tolerance for new ideas, willingness to use reason and evidence to solve problems, and willingness to see complexity in problems" (2005, 156). Mark, a volunteer in Honduras, illustrated aspects of this: "I have also learned not to be afraid of new and foreign places, or people. Although living in a completely different community, people are still people and I realized that in today's day and age it is important to understand, experience and question why certain communities run the way they do and why people live in the conditions they live in." This was especially evident in volunteers' reports about their growing suspicion of media.

Similarly, volunteers reported developing ways of understanding the world and an increased ability to see more options for organizing their lives. Volunteers' narratives suggest that with more points of reference they are able to see and critique from a more objective position alternative ways of behaving (an example of a more "complex" way of making meaning). As a result, returned volunteers often described feeling that they are making *decisions* about the way they are organizing their lives rather than simply following a path (e.g., choosing to attend college, or choosing to be a certain kind of neighbor or consumer, or desiring a certain type of community). In fact, having to mediate among competing perspectives during the year seemed to help volunteers recognize their own "voice" (Barnett 2007, 91) and perspectives on issues (e.g., "I now feel I have valid opinions to share . . . why not?"). These findings also suggest that volunteers, as William Perry (1970) outlined in his theory of cognitive development, are beginning to make commitments in their lives while also recognizing a pluralistic world.

Acting on these changes, it was common for volunteers to alter their course of study at college following their gap year. These modifications reflected new orientations, values, and meanings the volunteers made of themselves and the world—and their desires for how they wanted to contribute to the world. Discussing his new way of thinking about his degree, one volunteer said: "I just picked something I was naturally good at—rather than my interests." This finding resonates with Esther Suh's (2009) study on U.S. undergraduate volunteers who later tried to link their academic work to their volunteering experiences. Moreover, modifying college majors and vocational trajectories to match their own evolving interests and values suggests movement toward "self-authorship" and an emerging "internal voice" (Baxter Magolda 2009), which is discussed further in chapter 7. These changes, along with volunteers' new sense of purpose, perspectives on education, resilience, self-confidence, and interpersonal capacities, also suggest that gap years may improve college retention and graduation rates. We have already seen early research from the United Kingdom, United States and Australia that found that gap year students had higher academic motivation and better academic performance than their non-gap year peers—and that gap year students at Middlebury College in Vermont held a disproportionally high amount of leadership positions on campus (Buckles 2013; Clagett 2011; Crawford and Cribb 2012; Martin 2010).

On top of this, a stronger connection to the world and a greater understanding of its complexity also seemed to spur curiosity about the world. Volunteers' suggestion that the gap year helped to inculcate this desire—and helped them understand future experiences with greater depth—overlaps with John Dewey's "experiential continuum" and his promotion of experiences that deepened the desire to learn and built upon prior experiences (1938, 28). In addition, an increase in international awareness and desire to know more about the world is also cited across the literatures examining international experiences (e.g., study abroad, international service learning). A changing connection to the world also has some grounding in the intercultural learning literature. Specifically, these experiences of the volunteers resonate with the idea of an "evolving intercultural identity" found in Edward Taylor's (1994, 172) study, where "evolving intercultural identity" was described as a change in values, an increase in self-confidence, and a change in perspective, reflecting intercultural competence.

However, my findings partially contradict and add nuance to notions of intercultural learning that find that dissonance caused by "cultural disequilibrium . . . just lessens in intensity over time and as a participant becomes more interculturally competent" (Taylor 1993, 198). This was true in many respects, but often dissonance resumed when new situations arose that challenged volunteers in novel ways (e.g., experiencing the death of a child in their care and questioning anew the social arrangements in the world or a society's response to such an event). Regardless, the gap year was not just about cultural disequilibrium, but presented other challenges, as in interpersonal relationships with partners and host families and in the separation from volunteers' families of origin. These often involved intense emotions and dissonance for volunteers and helped change how they understood themselves and world.

Volunteers' experiences also sometimes led them to view their own opportunities in life and the civic structures in the world in a new light. For instance, as mentioned above, one volunteer said after his gap year he realized that: "I am a white man from England. If I can't make it then I am rubbish—many people there don't have these opportunities." This change resonates with Lise Sparrow's (2000) social constructivist view of cultural learning, which posits that "only members of dominant paradigms can have the luxurious illusion of objectivity or of a self which is free of social realities" (181). Gap years may have served to promote this type of learning; that is, the gap year provided the "context" for assisting volunteers in developing a critical awareness of, as Richard Kiely (2002, 315) puts it, the "socially constructed nature of identity relative to the poorer 'other.'" Volunteers' reported experiences also overlap with Freire's (1970, 27) process of "conscientization," by which adults "achieve a deepening awareness of both the sociocultural reality which shapes their lives and . . . their capacity to transform that reality through action upon it."

Similarly, this chapter outlines how dissonance occurred when volunteers came back to their home countries. Many had difficulty reconciling their new understandings with their lives back in Europe; some experienced their return to their home country as an ongoing struggle to resist certain cultural practices and views as they assimilated back to their old lives. In fact, many volunteers reported that returning home was more difficult than arriving in the gap year country for the first time. Many recalled feeling the "pressures" of resisting the "materialism" of the West and guilt from living with so much opportunity when their friends or children in their care during their year do not have the same opportunities. As one volunteer said a year after her gap year, "I still think about my children in the orphanage every day." Another said that "seeing the first world from a third world perspective" was "sickening." In addition, volunteers often felt "selfish" in their college lives, especially with their new recognition of inequalities and their potential to contribute to others' well-being—a "problem of potentiality," as one volunteer put it. On the surface, this might suggest a tension between the educational goal that some theorists propose—to "liberate" learners from that in which they are embedded (e.g., Freire 1970; Kegan 1994; Mezirow 2000)—and a new awareness of the world that can shackle one with guilt and continued dissonance. But at a deeper level, expanding one's understanding in a manner that leads one to action can itself be viewed as a fundamental form of liberation. Thus, as Alice Evans et al. (1987, 264–265) say of the ongoing struggle and guilt of the nonpoor when they encounter people living in poverty: "Facing the problem or recognizing the plight of the poor . . . the restlessness or feeling uncomfortable with that recognition . . . sustains a vision for the transformation of the conditions of the poor."

Part II / **Understanding the Gap Year**

6

Theorizing the Gap Year

In light of the lack of educational literature on gap years, I struggled with situating my findings regarding the effects of gap years on volunteers within the context of theory. As a researcher, I was challenged to develop an integrated framework that could encompass the diversity of the findings; no single paradigm seemed to capture them adequately. In this chapter, I present a theoretical framework that emerged from the findings that I developed as I analyzed the data.

The idea of *meaning-making* provides the fundamental conceptual bridge that unifies the volunteers' narratives of their gap years. Meaning-making refers to the "activity by which we shape a coherent meaning out of the raw material of our outer and inner experiencing" (Kegan 1994). Individuals make meaning in the space between their experiences and their reactions to them. As Robert Kegan explains:

> The activity of being a person is the activity of meaning-making. There is no
> feeling, no experience, no thought, no perception, independent of a meaning-
> making context in which it becomes a feeling, an experience, a thought, a
> perception, because we are the meaning-making context. (1982, 11)

Thus, the concept of meaning-making arises out of a position premised on the recognition that reality does not come to us preformed, simply waiting for us to copy a picture of it into our minds (Kegan 1994). Rather, our perceiving is simultaneously an act of conceiving, of interpreting (Kegan 1994). As a conceptual tool, meaning-making is broad enough to help capture the diversity of findings that emerge from volunteers' reports of their experiences.

Some researchers have used this concept in the study of adult and student development more generally, employing theories that rely on meaning-making as a central idea—such as *constructive-developmental theory* and *transformational learning*, defined below—and applying these theories in the context of particular experiences, such as international service learning and intercultural learning. More recently, Marcia Baxter Magolda (2009) offered a review and synthesis of college student development theory and literature on the activity of meaning-making, which I draw upon heavily in my theoretical framework.

Meaning-making in Developmental Literatures

The literature on human development in young adults has largely remained segregated along lines of theorizing: cognitive, moral, emotional, and so forth (Baxter Magolda 2009). However, these separations do not exist in practice; human development is more interrelated, and there are important aspects of development that occur at the intersections of these theories. Recently scholars have called for greater integration, with the aim of understanding development more holistically. Many have argued that the activity of meaning-making could be employed as a foundation that links and underpins much of the human development literature. Such an approach focuses on *how* we make meaning—the processes through which we come to understand the world, rather than on the *particular* meanings we make (Baxter Magolda 2009).

As Jean Piaget (1950) described, people use a set of assumptions to guide how they understand—how they make meaning—of their experience. As individuals are exposed to new information and experiences that create *cognitive dissonance*, or a psychological tension caused by trying to hold conflicting beliefs, they first attempt to incorporate the new data in their current way of understanding. However, if the new information or data cannot fit within existing structures or frames of understanding, they create a new, more complex structure through the process of *accommodation*. In the language of meaning-making, this process results in growth toward more complex meaning-making capabilities (Boes et al. 2010). A similar notion of development toward increasingly complex ways of forming judgments also undergirds the major works on the development of moral reasoning (Gilligan 1982; Kohlberg 1981) and psychosocial development (Chickering and Reisser 1993).

Constructive-developmental theory speaks to the activity of meaning-making directly, explicitly defining development as greater complexity of meaning-making (Kegan 1994). According to this theory, development both unfolds naturally and is stimulated by the limitations of existing ways of making meaning

(Nicolaides and Yorks 2007). The extent to which a person moves to more complex principles of mental organization depends on the nature and intensity of the challenges confronting her, her individual characteristics, and the degree of support available for facing the challenge of reorganizing meaning-making (Baxter Magolda 2009; Kegan 1994).

Viewed through constructive-developmental theory, meaning-making integrates the three major realms of development: cognitive, intrapersonal, and interpersonal. The *cognitive dimension* focuses on how one's understanding of knowledge and the ways it is gained contribute to shaping one's meaning-making system. The *intrapersonal dimension* focuses on the parallel influences of how one understands one's own beliefs, values, and sense of self. Finally, the *interpersonal dimension* of meaning-making concerns how one views oneself in relationship to other people (their views, values, behaviors, etc.) and makes choices in social situations (Baxter Magolda 2009). Kegan argues that development in all three dimensions is required for a person to be fully able to use her skills, and Baxter Magolda argues that all three developmental dimensions are central to learning (Baxter Magolda 2009; Kegan 1994). Moreover, Kegan has developed a model on which development in meaning-making progresses through a series of "orders of consciousness" (1994).

Baxter Magolda (2001) explored Kegan's (1994) theory in a longitudinal study of college students and young adults. She suggested that what Kegan describes as the "third order of consciousness" is the most prevalent meaning-making structure among college students of typical age. This third order is characterized by making meaning through concrete relationships to which one's own interests are subordinated (Kegan 1994). In this order, relationships generally define identity, and a person lacks developed capacities for negotiating their conflicting demands. As Baxter Magolda (1999a) puts it, a person engages in "formulaic" meaning-making, in which a socialized perspective dominates. She contends that some college students make meaning at the fourth order, however, through "foundational" meaning-making (1999a), which is centrally characterized by self-authorship.

Underpinned by maturation (increased complexity) in all three developmental domains (interpersonal, intrapersonal, and cognitive), self-authorship is a way of making meaning that rests on an "ability to construct knowledge in a contextual world, an ability to construct an internal identity separate from external influences, and an ability to engage in relationships without losing one's internal identity" (Baxter Magolda 1999b, 12). In other words, there is an emergence of an "internal voice to coordinate external influence and manage one's life" (Baxter Magolda 2009, 628). She explains:

> As young adults begin to compose their own realities and re-center into adult
> contexts, they renegotiate the relationship of their internal voices and external
> influence. External forces, initially in the foreground of meaning-making, move
> to the background as internal forces move to the foreground of meaning-making.
> Thus, the internal voice becomes the coordinator of external influence. (2009,
> 625)

This transition from external to internal definition has been identified by other scholars. Jennifer Tanner, Jeffrey Arnett, and Julie Leis, for instance, deem this period "emerging adulthood," during which young people are gaining self-sufficiency and recentering from childhood to contexts that "nourish adult interdependence" (2008, 38). Similarly, Sharon Parks noted:

> In the years from seventeen to thirty a distinctive mode of meaning-making can
> emerge . . . [that] includes (1) becoming critically aware of one's own composing
> of reality, (2) self-consciously participating in an on-going dialogue toward truth,
> and (3) cultivating a capacity to respond—to act—in ways that are satisfying and
> just. (2000, 6)

Baxter Magolda posits that students making a transition to self-authorship are at a "crossroads" (1999b, 38). During this transitional period dominated by "tensions and unresolved conflicts between their developing internal voices and external influences, students gradually question formulas increasingly incongruent with developing internal values" (Abes et al. 2007, 5). In Baxter Magolda's (2001) study, she found that self-authorship was often catalyzed by one of two kinds of experiences: participants either had to make a decision for which there was no formula for success or they realized they were sufficiently unhappy in their present situations to start making changes, but they had to figure out what sorts of changes could be made and how to make them on their own.

Based on this data, Baxter Magolda suggested that college students were likely not developing self-authorship, because institutions of higher education did not provide sufficiently provocative experiences—experiences that disrupted students' equilibrium such that they felt compelled to consider and begin to construct new conceptions of self (Baxter Magolda 2001; Pizzolato 2005). According to Baxter Magolda, universities too readily supply students with formulas for success, so students do not have to develop self-authored ways of knowing (2001).

However, Jane Pizzolato found that high-risk students in college—those who often came from low-income backgrounds and were the first to attend college in their families—had begun to develop self-authored ways of knowing before entering college (2003). Thus, she concluded that students' self-authorship development seems to be affected by "privilege," or having readily accessible formulas for success (2003). Lack of privilege often placed students in situations where achieving their "possible selves" as college students required them to self-author by creating their own formulas for success (2003). By contrast, higher levels of privilege appeared to work in just the opposite way: these students had excessive support that often crossed the line into protection. That is, they were protected from having to figure out how to apply to or pay for college and from considering the implications of attending college on their sense of self. Consequently, "highly privileged students were kept from opportunities where they could have more fully developed self-authoring ways of knowing" (Pizzolato 2003, 808).

The field of student development is converging around the concept of self-authorship as a desired developmental outcome (Evans et al. 2009), and Patricia King and Marcia Baxter Magolda (1996) even declare that the "achievement of self-authorship should be heralded as a central purpose of higher education." Generally, the primary contribution of developmental theories is in their accounts of how people develop more complex and comprehensive ways of making sense of themselves and their experiences (McCauley et. al. 2006).

Meaning-making in Transformational Learning Theories

Meaning-making is also embedded in the conceptual vocabulary of transformational learning theory, which Jack Mezirow originally developed in the 1970s. He argues that we make meaning of our experiences through acquired frames of reference—sets of orientating assumptions and expectations with "cognitive, affective, and conative dimensions . . . that shape, delimit, and sometimes distort our understanding" and that we derive from our social context (2009, 29). Mezirow contends that these assumptions can vary in type, including sociolinguistic, moral-ethical, psychological, and aesthetic dispositions, as well as our political orientations, understanding of gender roles, and religious and philosophical beliefs.

How do these assumptions develop over time? According to Mezirow, "We transform our frames of reference by becoming critically reflective of our assumptions to make them more dependable when the beliefs and understandings they generate become problematic" (2009, 29–30). He posits that these changes in our frames of reference, or transformations, typically occur when we confront "disorienting dilemmas" triggered by a life crisis or major life transition. They can also come about because of an accumulation of changes in our points of view about more particular phenomena over a period of time (Mezirow 2000). Transformational learning theory thus offers a somewhat greater focus than constructive-developmental theory on one's *particular* made meanings (such as changes in one's assumptions about one's home country or the nature of community), rather than the *capacities* or *methods* for meaning-making highlighted by the developmental theories outlined above.

However, even though Mezirow does not speak directly in developmental terms, there is a clear synergy between this account and the constructive-developmental notion of meaning-making. Mezirow maintains that transformative learning theory demands that we strive to "think critically about assumptions supporting one's perspectives and to develop critically reflective judgment in discourse regarding one's beliefs, values, feelings, and self-concepts" (2009, 29). This is similar in kind to the process of development in one's "organizing principle" described by Kegan (1994). In addition, the process of transformation illustrated by Mezirow hinges on "how we learn to negotiate and act on our own purposes, values, feelings, and meanings rather than those we have uncritically assimilated from others" (2000, 8). This recalls the process of moving away from reliance on external authority and toward self-authorship that is the central focus of Kegan's (1994) and Baxter Magolda's (2009) constructive-developmental theories. Indeed, the "provocative moments" or "crossroads" that self-authorship scholars discuss are similar to Mezirow's transformational learning theory's "disorienting dilemmas." At the intersection of these various terms is a common concept: a disequilibrium of meanings that challenges learners to reflect on dissonant situations and make decisions that guide future action.

Of course, theoretical discussion of the processes of development and transformation naturally prompts the question what individuals or institutions can *do* to facilitate such growth. Arthur Zajonc (2010) engages this question from the perspective of higher education institutions in particular, arguing that integrative education is necessary to facilitate students' meaning-making. Specifically, Zajonc suggests that an "intense, sustained, active, and experiential modality of engagement is required" for this purpose (2010, 105). He believes that deep changes in our underlying assumptions take both time and exposure of a particular kind:

> In order to change, we must first find ways to temporarily inhabit other ways of being and knowing, exploring them for a time, trying alternatives on for size. Therefore, a prerequisite for an enduring shift in meaning-making is that we are able to place ourselves in the world of others. Empathetic and imaginative knowing does exactly this; we repeatedly live others' lives, experience their joys and sorrows, their trials and successes. (2010, 106)

Zajonc argues that curriculum choices should be informed by this understanding of the stimuli for meaning-making. In particular: "The methods by which we challenge our students, open them to change, will vary, but to be successful they should include cross-cultural studies in which worldviews radically different from their own are encountered and appreciated" (2010, 105–106). As discussed later in this book, the findings suggest that international volunteering gap years may offer participants these opportunities.

The exploration of the literature above also suggests other early clues as to the ways in which gap years could foster development and transformational learning. In addition to exposing students to "radically" new perspectives, the international volunteering gap year may also often present the "disorienting dilemmas" emphasized by Mezirow (2000). Similarly, Kegan asserts that transitions from one order of consciousness to the next can be catalyzed when the "life curriculum" one faces becomes qualitatively more challenging (1994). Kegan posits that "people grow best when they continuously experience an ingenious blend of support and challenge; the rest is commentary" (1994, 42). International volunteering gap years will typically challenge participants in various ways, but it certainly remains an open question whether they get this balance right. In chapter 8, which discusses designing the gap year, I will consider the task of finding the optimal level of challenge and support for each volunteer.

An Expanded Conception of Meaning-making

It is not surprising that gap years have not been examined in light of transformational learning theory or the student development frameworks I have discussed. These literatures originated and are often sustained by student affairs professionals and adult educators in the United States, where gap years have historically been less common. Student development theory and transforma-

tional learning theory often do not meet even within the United States literature, presumably due to boundaries between academic domains. As Nancy Evans
et al. (2009) argue:

> Student development educators must recognize the need to investigate learning
> theory, particularly Mezirow's (2000, 372) transformational learning and other
> theories mainly found in the literature of adult development and education. . . . A
> consideration of integration and intersection of all parts of student development
> provides a warrant for new and creative ways to examine the whole.

The framework developed in this chapter is one such attempt, albeit a prelimi-
nary one, to provide a "new and creative way to examine the whole."

In the course of analyzing the data, I repeatedly attempted to place the findings of this study within one specific theory. However, it became increasingly
clear that to fully capture the volunteers' narratives in this holistic study a wider
perspective was required. First, although transformational learning theory focuses some attention on changes in particular meanings and viewpoints, as an
adult learning theory it is limited in its ability to place these changes in a longitudinal perspective of developmental movement toward more complex meaning-
making capacities. In other words, without a life span focus, transformational
learning theory fails to integrate changes in meaning-making in one's developmental journey. Examining the developmental changes that volunteers' narratives
highlighted seems critically important to understanding their experiences.

At the same time, as a broad developmental theory, constructive-developmental theory does not offer enough focus on the particular meanings that we
make. Its focus on not *what* we think but *how* we think erects a boundary that
limits our understanding of who people actually are and who they become. After
all, several people may have the same capacity to "self-author," but they may
author a wide range of different selves. In addition, constructive-developmental
theory does not offer an in-depth understanding of how particular shifts in viewpoint come about or how they can be facilitated in educational settings—both of
which transformational learning can help provide. Given the mutual limitations
of these theories and the variety of experiences in the volunteers' narratives, I
aim to integrate the fields of student development theory and adult learning (i.e.,
transformational learning) under the umbrella concept of meaning-making. A
suitable conception of meaning-making requires a focus both on how people
make meaning and what meanings they actually make.

Civic Meaning-making

This dual focus on meaning-making capacities and made meanings represents a broadening of our attention. At the same time, it will be useful to narrow our focus in a second dimension in order to furnish an organizing principle that structures the themes in volunteers' narratives. As I described in the previous chapters, volunteers developed their meaning-making capacities and made new meanings in many different spheres. But many of these changes in meaning-making were connected by certain common threads.

In particular, the gap year experience often seemed to promote volunteers' development as participants in public life, of life in community with others. On the one hand, volunteers' narratives suggest that they developed greater meaning-making capacities tuned to participation with others in social life—including increased openness and empathy, interest in the wider world, and contextual and critical orientations toward knowledge. On the other hand, the narratives also suggest that volunteers' particular made meanings and viewpoints evolved as well, including with respect to their conceptions of themselves, others, and what they wanted out of life. Their notions of community and common good developed toward seeing unknown others as part of "humanity" and showing greater concern for their welfare, as well as placing a greater importance on relationships and less on material possessions in the "good life." Further, volunteers' ideas about how society could be constructed or how they could help to enable people to pursue this good life—for instance, through public policies or more involvement in civic affairs—evolved as well.

Thus it will help to integrate a third field of literature that speaks to these substantive areas in particular—civic education—with our developing notions of meaning-making. By seeing civic development through this lens, we may better understand how flourishing public life—both locally and globally—is underpinned by complex meaning-making capacities *and* particular meanings about oneself and the world. Further, by integrating civic education into this paradigm, we may be better able to understand the processes through which these foundational capacities and perspectives change. In this book, I use the idea of *civic meaning-making* to capture this particular combination of capacities and understandings.

In the sections below, I consider the literature on civic education and cosmopolitanism. The findings of this study suggest that cosmopolitanism was one axis on which civic meaning-making occurred, so it is important to review the theoretical literature in this area. I do not intend for this section to be an exhaustive overview of either civic education or broader notions of citizenship. Philosophers and political theorists have long debated the qualities that make for a good citizen, and I merely present a sketch of some of these ideas. I reserve most of the work of situating my findings in this theoretical context until the next chapter.

Civic Education

From antiquity to the modern era, scholars have looked to education as a means of forming able citizens. Indeed, it is often said that democratic citizenship rests on effective education. Recently many educational policy-makers have called for an increased focus on preparing young people to be citizens in an international community—to have the competences, desires, and perspectives to contribute not only to their community or country but also to the larger world (Welikala and Watkins 2008). In ancient Greece, Plato saw the formation of human beings and citizens as inextricably bound; in his view, a virtuous citizen is simply a virtuous person acting in the public or political sphere (Crittenden 2007). Plato believed that education was central in developing such virtue in people. In the *Laws*, Plato proposes: "Ask in general what great benefit the state derives from the training by which it educates its citizens, and the reply will be perfectly straightforward. The good education they have received will make them good men" (Crittenden 2007, 641b7–10).

John Dewey continued this discussion in the twentieth century, articulating education's role in forming the combination of virtues and perspectives required by good citizens (Crittenden 2007). As Dewey saw it, democracy is something more than simply every citizen having the right to vote; it is a "way of relational living in which the decisions and actions of one citizen must be understood in terms of their influence on the lives of others" (Rhoads 2000, 38). Dewey wrote in 1916:

> Democracy has to be born anew every generation and education is its midwife. Moreover, it is only education which can guarantee widespread community of interest and aim. In a complex society, ability to understand and sympathize with the operations and lot of others is a condition of common purpose which only education can procure. The external differences of pursuit and experience are so very great in our complicated industrial civilization, that men will not see across

and through the walls which separate them, unless they have been trained to do so. (1916/1980, 139)

Likewise, democracy, as Robert Rhoads (2000) posits, demands the development of a "caring self"—people with the capacities to understand others and a particular orientation toward improving the well-being of others. In developing a notion of *civic* meaning-making, I mean to invoke a similarly broad understanding. Although the words "civic" and "citizenship" can, especially in public policy debates, have more narrow connotations concerning voting and fulfilling our political obligations, I think of civic life as in community with others, or public life.

Both Dewey and John Stuart Mill thought it was important for young people to develop as citizens by participating in their own governance, expanding their notions of community and the contributions they can make to it (Dewey 1938; Mill 1972). To implement his ideas in schools, Dewey believed that we need to:

> make each one of our schools an embryonic community life, active with types of occupations that reflect the life of the larger society and permeated throughout with the spirit of art, history, and science. When the school introduces and trains each child of society into membership within such a little community, saturating him with the spirit of service, and providing him with the instruments of effective self-directing we shall have the deepest and best guarantee of a larger society which is worthy, lovely, and harmonious. (1889/2001, 22)

The central challenge of civic education is discerning which capacities or virtues we want in our citizens and how education could go about fostering these forms of development. In particular, there is a tension between the need for democracies to "perpetuate" their systems, rules, and institutions, and the need to "challenge those very systems and rules" (Crittenden 2007). Thus Jack Crittenden argues that "civic education in a democracy, though not in every kind of regime, must prepare citizens to participate in and thereby perpetuate the system and at the same time prepare them to challenge what they see as inequities and injustice within that system." Other writers (e.g., Freire 1970) have called attention to this tension in the curriculum of civic education and its aim at perpetuating democracy and existing systems, while at the same time providing students with skills and desires to challenge them.

Any successful republic depends on the intellectual and moral virtues of its people (Battistoni 1985). Leaders need the prudence to discern the common good and the integrity to promote it when support is lacking; citizens need the empathy to put the common good above individual interests, the civility to deliberate openly about what that means, and the self-discipline, moderation, and justice to live accordingly. Cultivating these can be difficult, however, and elsewhere I have discussed the limits of focusing too much on the intellectual and theoretical elements of our character formation and behavior (O'Shea 2011). Even if students have studied a theory of justice or ethics or political science, this often does not move them to act. It does not develop the appreciation for a way of being that can only come from lived experiences. Thus I have suggested that intellectual discussion and voluntary service are parallel halves that are each insufficient to cultivate a disposition for benevolence. What is needed is to align higher education's efforts at character development through experiential influences like voluntary service and relationships, on the one hand, with intellectual engagement and critical self-reflection, on the other (O'Shea 2011).

Janet Eyler and Dwight Giles (1999) have proposed an instructive theory of citizenship development, informed by a landmark study of service learning for college students. In their assessment, citizenship requires five core elements: values, knowledge, skills, efficacy, and commitment. I use these five elements as a structuring device in developing a fuller (though not exhaustive) account of the abilities and understandings that civic meaning-making might entail.

The first element, *values*, consists in a "sense of social responsibility, and engagement, or feeling connected to the community" that can "provide a powerful motivation for involvement" (Eyler and Giles 1999, 157). The values that undergird citizenship involve a conception of the common good and of the good life, which respects and supports the functioning of others in public life. As Norman Nie et al. (1996, 14) argue, democratic citizenship requires that individuals value the collective enterprises of their community. Although Eyler and Giles do not conceive of their theory in terms of meaning-making, these values can be viewed as one set of particular made meanings about what is good and desirable in the world. They amount to an "others-oriented" viewpoint, in which the interests and well-being of others are valued. But the utility of these particular beliefs or meanings for effective citizenship rests on the possession of certain meaning-making capacities as well. It presumes that a citizen is sufficiently reflective to *know* her own values and thus to identify her preferences in democratic community life when contributing to deliberation over the common good.

The second element identified by Eyler and Giles is a kind of *knowledge*. In particular, they highlight the need for some specific knowledge about public policy or the other issues confronting individuals as participants in community life, as well the capacity to make sense of it. They write, "It is not enough to feel committed to community. Students also need the expertise and cognitive capacity to make intelligent decisions about what needs to be done" (1999, 158). Regarding their third component, *skills*, Eyler and Giles maintain that it is not sufficient to "have a sophisticated understanding of social issues and public policy options" because people "may be unaware of how to proceed to make a difference" (1999, 160). Here Eyler and Giles emphasize the need for the capacities to act on one's made meanings in the world, including social skills. More broadly, these surely include the interpersonal capacities required to understand an issue from another's point of view. The fourth element of Eyler and Giles' framework is *efficacy*, or the feeling of self-belief and self-confidence that one can make a difference. Here, they are capturing a particular made meaning about oneself; that is, as a confident and efficacious self. Eyler and Giles' final component is *commitment*, understood as the sense of investment in a community or wider society and the actions one takes as a result. This commitment necessarily rests on a particular set of made meanings as well, in the form of a conception of one's community and of one's role as a participant in it. This element is especially important today given some social scientists' observations of declining senses of community life, social trust, and social capital in the United States and elsewhere and the deleterious effects on democracy and public life (see, for instance, Putnam, 2000).

Together, an understanding of these five elements helps to illuminate the interplay of both meaning-making capacities—intrapersonal, interpersonal, and cognitive—and particular made meanings in sustaining democratic and community life. These capacities and convictions together form important aspects of what I have described as civic meaning-making. The concept thus heeds Richard Pring's (2008) admonition that while a "sense of community and democracy" is an important goal of education, it should not be set apart from or pursued to the exclusion of a broader "range of understandings, skills, qualities, practical capacities, virtues and attitudes which make up the whole person."

Cosmopolitanism in Civic Meaning-making

As seen in the discussion of civic education above, a variety of qualities contribute to successful functioning in public life. In this section, I explore another cluster of such qualities, and hence another possible element of civic meaning-making, which can be grouped under the banner of *cosmopolitanism*.

Responding to mounting internationalization, educational thinkers have proposed that educators direct more of their efforts toward fostering greater international awareness and intercultural competency (Welikala and Watkins 2008). Thus Martha Nussbaum (1996, 9) has called for efforts to inculcate a sense of cosmopolitanism in young people—to educate them to be global citizens who "make all human beings part of our community of dialogue and concern." She explains:

> The accident of where one is born is just that, an accident; any human being might have been born in any nation. Recognizing this, we should not allow differences of nationality or class or ethnic membership or even gender to erect barriers between us and our fellow human beings. We should recognize humanity—and its fundamental ingredients, reason and moral capacity—wherever it occurs, and give that community of humanity our first allegiance. (1997, 58–59)

According to Sharon Todd (2008), such appeals to cosmopolitanism reflect the demands of an increasingly internationalized world and seek to "counteract the very devastating realities of social dissolution that plague societies throughout the world and unite us under a banner of respect for what we share as human beings."

There are certainly objections to the normative claims of cosmopolitanism, which may bear on whether cosmopolitan orientations should be regarded as a valuable component of civic meaning-making. The most powerful of these criticisms direct their attention to people's desires and abilities to give preferential attention to those immediately around them—particularly in their local community and nation—instead of affording equal concern to all humans. Scholars also object that it is simply not psychologically possible to be a genuine cosmopolitan—that human beings must have stronger attachments "toward members of their own state or nation, and that attempts to disperse attachments to fellow-citizens in order to honor a moral community with human beings as such will cripple our sensibilities" (Kleingeld and Brown 2006).

A more moderate cosmopolitanism may defuse these objections. Such a view can insist not on *identical* concern for all humans, but rather a baseline favorable, positively motivating attitude toward all; this leaves room for some special attitudes toward a fellow citizen (Kleingeld and Brown 2006). Even Nussbaum grants that students may, consistent with cosmopolitanism, consider themselves partly determined by their specific commitments to their religion, country, and race. However, they must also learn to recognize humanity where they encounter it and to identify the commonality of ends even when this is obscured by cultural difference (Nussbaum 1996, 21; Papastephanou 2002, 73).

One might object that this respect of humanity as such promotes a sense of cultural relativism that hinders moral progress by disallowing the claim that some actions are wrong even if they are endorsed by the local culture. However, as Kwame Anthony Appiah (2006) responds, cultural differences only need be respected insofar as they are not harmful to people and in no way conflict with our universal concern for every human's life and well-being.

With these concerns set aside, moderate cosmopolitanism does offer an insightful and useful perspective on what makes for valuable civic meaning-making. Indeed, Nussbaum suggests a broadly developmental understanding of the *psychology of concern*—that as we develop further, our circle of care expands and we are able to include others beyond those around us and our compatriots within it, until it encompasses those in other nations and of other backgrounds. This clearly echoes constructive-developmental theories that describe our increasingly complex meaning-making capacities.

To help identify the specific meaning-making capacities required for cosmopolitan thought and action, I follow Nussbaum in recognizing three essential and mutually beneficial capacities of a "world citizen" (1997). First among these is the capacity for "critical examination of oneself and one's tradition—for living, following Socrates, what we may call the 'examined life'" (1997, 9). Nussbaum argues for independence in thought: that one must take reasoning in one's own hands, form one's own beliefs (in concert with others), and have a confidence that one can engage with issues. This demands a commitment to reflect on our worldviews and self-understanding. Connecting this call with the developing theoretical framework, we can see Nussbaum as urging a way of making meaning that echoes ideas of self-authorship in constructive-developmental theory and "critical reflection" on our assumptions in transformational learning theory.

The second element is the ability of a person to see herself "not simply as a citizen of some local region or group, but also and above all, as a human being bound to all other human beings by ties of recognition and concern . . . Cultivating our humanity in a complex, interlocking world involves understanding the ways in which common needs and aims are differently realized in different circumstances" (1999, 10). This calls for knowledge and study of other cultures, places, and ways of being—which, as Nussbaum observes, is undermined by traditionalists who "resist the idea that we should cultivate our perceptions of the

human through a confrontation with cultures and groups that we have traditionally regarded as unequal."

The final element, and perhaps the most important, is the capacity for "narrative imagination." This, as Nussbaum sees it, is the "ability to think what it
might be like to be in the shoes of a person different from oneself, to be an intelligent reader of that person's story, and to understand the emotions and wishes
and desires that someone so placed might have" (1999, 10–11). This cognitive
and affective meaning-making capacity helps us to not be "obtuse" toward other
people and ways of being—and also to reflect on our own ways of being. She
suggests that we have to cultivate an "imaginative capacity to enter the lives of
people of other nations" (1999, 294). Although Nussbaum acknowledges that
there are other elements to effective cosmopolitan citizenship as well, such as
scientific knowledge, these three elements are primary in helping us to respect
the humanity of others and cultivate our own.

Summary

In this chapter I have outlined the theoretical framework that I engage with and
build on in the book, centering on the concepts of meaning-making and of civic
meaning-making in particular. This framework contributes to the fields of student development theory, adult learning, and civic education by building a conceptual bridge through the concept of meaning-making that connects both the
capacities to form understandings of the world and the particular views that are
thereby made. It also lays a foundation for examining the findings of this research, which, broadly construed, suggest that gap year participants developed
toward richer civic meaning-making.

7

Developing Citizens

A socially cohesive and economically vibrant U.S. democracy and a viable,
just global community require informed, engaged, open-minded, and socially
responsible people committed to the common good and practiced in "doing"
democracy.

—*National Task Force on Civic Learning and Democratic Engagement*

In review, the previous chapters have offered an in-depth study of the gap year
experience for participants. They attempted to illustrate what was meaningful
for volunteers—the reasons why they undertook the gap year experience and
the ways they believed it had affected them. Regarding motivations, I found
that, despite many industry appeals to altruism, volunteers tended to have
largely egoistic motivations for undertaking their international volunteering gap
year. However, as time progressed, their motivations to stay on and continue
their work until the end of their placement tended to become more altruistic,
rooted in a concern about the well-being of those in their care.

Volunteers experienced a broad range of changes stemming from their gap
years. I have grouped these changes around broad and interrelated themes: intrapersonal (i.e., their sense of self), interpersonal (i.e., their sense of self in
relation to others), civic and religious (e.g., changes in ideas of community), and
finally, intellectual practices and future plans (e.g., moving to a more relative
understanding of the world). Together, these themes help to illustrate the significant ways in which volunteers experienced the gap year as having influenced
them.

I have also sought to situate these findings within educational theory. In
order to accommodate the diversity of findings, I developed a theoretical framework based upon the activity of meaning-making. This framework bridges two
kinds of theories—constructive developmental and transformational learning—
which I detailed in chapter 6. In this chapter, I build on that foundation by exploring how the gap year, by offering novel challenges for the volunteers, served
to catalyze changes both in the meanings volunteers made of the world (e.g., the
role of religion) and in their capacities for more complex meaning-making

schemes (e.g., their ability to place their experiences in a relative light). As such, the gap year also served to promote development toward increasingly "self-authored" ways of making meaning and fostered civic meaning-making of the kind we considered in the previous chapter.

The Gap Year and Changes in Meaning

The gap year encouraged changes and development in volunteers by engaging them in different ways of living. As we saw in the narratives, volunteers often sought the experience because they were somehow unsatisfied with their current state. In the gap year, they had the opportunity to engage in cognitive dissonance and live a very different life, "trying on" other ways of understanding the world—of making meaning—through their daily experiences. Such opportunities to "try on" other ways of making sense of the world, living the life of another, are key to the process of reforming meaning-making schemes (Mezirow 2000; Zajonc 2010). As Parker Palmer (1980) wrote, regarding transformational learning: "We do not think our way into a new kind of living; rather, we live our way into a new kind of thinking." The long-term nature of the gap year and the roles occupied by volunteers facilitated this process, by allowing them to work toward a life integrated with the local community. As one volunteer, who lived in a small aboriginal village in Guyana in his year, said: "I changed because I lived as a local . . . I lived as a villager so I was able to see the world from that perspective."

Renegotiating meaning-making schemes was an emotional process as well as a rational one. This provides general support for Elizabeth Tisdell's (2001) and Richard Kiely's (2004) arguments that emotional engagement is an important condition for remaking meaning and that pedagogy that integrates affective elements can be more effective at catalyzing changes. As the volunteers' stories illustrated, the gap year experiences can stimulate very intense emotions, especially as volunteers build relationships with those around them. These relationships helped volunteers to learn more about the culture, put a "human face" on or "personalize the third world," and see the world from another's perspective—in the end, becoming more concerned about the well-being of others. This mirrors Noddings' (1984, 14) argument that moral education involves building relationships through a deep exploration of otherness: "When we see the other's reality as a possibility for us, we must act to eliminate the intolerable. . . . When I am in this sort of relationship with another, when the other's reality becomes a real possibility for me, I care."

My research supports previous studies that indicate dissonance can play an important role in catalyzing the remaking of meanings. As shown in the narratives, gap year experiences can offer occasions for such dissonance by encouraging sustained engagement with novel stimuli that do not sit easily with existing understandings of the world. This dissonance was fueled by tension between aspects of the new culture, ways of being, and the volunteers' previous experience— an experience similar in kind to that observed by Kiely (2004) in his study of an international service-learning program. Some of the study's findings also fit naturally with Jack Mezirow's (2000) theory of the role of "disorienting dilemmas" as triggers for the process of "perspective transformation," as well as with theories of intercultural learning that see "culture shock" as a catalyst for significant learning and growth (Adler 1975; Bennett 1993; Kim 2001).

The important role of dissonance is illustrated, for instance, by the volunteer who realized that his ideas about Islam were wrong after working with Muslim children. He said that this "opened my mind to criticism" and led him to question "what else could be wrong?" In this case, the dissonance was experienced as a relatively sudden breakdown in the ability to accommodate new experiences by appeal to established understandings. However, the narratives also reflect that productive dissonance often manifested itself only through sustained immersion and an extended experience of attempting to inhabit another's perspective. For example, one volunteer, Mark, said he "changed because I lived as a local"; he saw the world "from the perspective of a villager" and thereby came to see our ways of being and social arrangements as "social constructs." This echoes Arthur Zajonc's (2010) and Palmer's (1980) claims about the conditions for transformational learning. As Zajonc puts it, a "prerequisite for an enduring shift in meaning-making is that we are able to place ourselves in the world of others . . . we repeatedly live others' lives, experience their joys and sorrows, their trials and successes" (2010, 106).

For many of the volunteers, these changes happened without their noticing, as Zajonc (2010) also suggests is typical of transformational learning. Often volunteers realized the extent to which they had changed only when a person pointed it out to them on their return or when they noticed differences in how they constructed meaning and how their peers did after returning home. A volunteer who had returned to the United Kingdom remarked: "I have progressively come to realize just how significant an impact the environment of Chenapou village and the people within it have had upon my personality." Likewise, a volunteer who was in northwest China for his year recalled: "I didn't notice any change in myself over the year—but my family and friends did when I came back. They said the way I speak, the way I stand, the way I hold myself, was so different. I didn't think about how I was changing, it was just from others noticing it."

Volunteers encountered dissonance throughout the gap year experience. Initially, as volunteers assimilated into the local culture, the differences they faced were striking, but these often became more familiar over time. However, as volunteers continued questioning and reflecting on different elements of the experiences, and as they had new experiences, they often reengaged with difference. It is interesting to note that assimilation into the local culture often led volunteers to experience their *country of origin* as a new and disorienting place when they returned—and that triggered further dissonance and identity work as volunteers continued to question and reflect on their lives back home.

Mezirow and other transformational learning theorists have argued that the most significant learning experiences involve critical self-reflection—"reassessing the way we have posed problems and reasons we have for our own orientation to perceiving, knowing, believing, feeling, and acting" (Kiely 2002; Mezirow 2000). This element of reflection is also emphasized by service-learning theorists. For example, Robert Rhoads (1997, 185) contends that "service without a reflective component fails to be forward looking, fails to be concerned about the community beyond the present, and in essence fails as community service."

Although gap years do not often have formal reflective components, the volunteers in this study used a variety of means to process the intrapersonal, interpersonal, and cognitive dimensions of their experiences—often assisted by their volunteer partners. The gap year experience allowed ample space and time for reflection, something that shorter-term programs may not be as able to provide. However, as seen in the earlier discussion of difficulties volunteers experience after their gap years, some participants—especially those who were particularly busy in their placements—recalled feeling that they were not able to reflect upon their experience, which often caused problems when they returned home and to college life. For instance, Amy reported that she "didn't really reflect on [her] year while overseas" and said she was returning to India the summer after her first year in college in hopes of reconciling the tensions between her "two homes." Furthermore, volunteers who experienced intense emotional and moral "trauma" often felt they had insufficient opportunities to deal with these experiences, in part because peers in their home countries did not provide a sufficient outlet for discussing their gap year.

It is also clear that volunteers varied in the sophistication of their analysis of the local culture and social problems, in the extent to which they encountered these problems, and in the interests they took in their work or host community more generally. Volunteers in orphanages, for instance, often reported less exposure to the larger community and to civic issues beyond their immediate work than other volunteers, such as those who were teachers in rural communities. This highlights the role that context can play in influencing how a person engages with dissonance and in catalyzing the remaking of meanings, something that transformational learning and self-authorship literatures have been criticized for overlooking. Further, my research into gap years extends previous theories and empirical research by illustrating how different forms of dissonance—the "life curriculum" in Robert Kegan's words (e.g., professional roles, living situations, environment, etc.)—and the corresponding challenges of the gap year can contribute to meaning-making changes.

The Gap Year and Change in Ways of Making Meaning

In addition to suggesting that they had changed understandings of the world, volunteers' narratives also signaled development in the *ways* they make meaning. As seen in the previous chapters, these more complex ways of making meaning had multiple dimensions—cognitive, interpersonal, and intrapersonal.

Cognitively, volunteers reported increased capacities to understand a wider breadth of issues and a more critical orientation toward knowledge, relying more on themselves for the formation of their viewpoints. Interpersonally, volunteers expressed a greater capacity to develop relationships with people different from themselves, as well as to empathize with others. Intrapersonally, volunteers often felt that they developed greater capacities to understand themselves and became less reliant on the perspectives of others. Thus, for example, many came to view the direction of their lives, such as going to college, as a decision, rather than as the result of following an "academic treadmill" or external pressures. Mark, a volunteer in Honduras, said that "I learnt to relax and question what I actually want from life, instead of doing things for other people all the time." Another volunteer said: "I have certainly become more confident. I feel more secure in my own opinions and better able to formulate and develop my own views on issues."

Indeed, development in one of these three domains may have helped in developing the others. One paradigmatic pattern of meaning-making changes, described in Susan Jones and Eliza Abes (2004, 163), might usefully be applied here. In particular, meeting new people may have encouraged the dissonance needed for greater cognitive complexity and facilitated volunteers' abilities to develop their own perspectives. At the same time, greater cognitive complexity may have increased a volunteer's receptivity to new perspectives, which together may have helped volunteers better understand themselves and move toward an internally defined self. As with changes in volunteers' more particular made meanings, changes in their meaning-making capacities also seemed to come about through engagement with numerous experiences that were distinct from their current understandings (e.g., of religion) and demanded more complex ways of understanding or acting in the world (e.g., necessitating the empathy to understand another person's needs in caring for him or her).

In addition, these capacities complement each other as factors in a person's decision-making. For example, when trying to make meaning of a situation and determine what is the morally right response, a volunteer may now be better able to reflect about what he or she believes in (through greater intrapersonal understanding), how it may affect others (through greater empathy and interpersonal capabilities), or the relative merits of making a particular choice from a wider variety of perspectives (cognitive dimensions).

The developments in meaning-making capacities that were evident in volunteers' reports echo Kegan's understanding of "growth of the mind" as "liberating ourselves from that in which we were embedded, making what was subject into object so that we can 'have it' rather than 'be had' by it" (1994, 34). These developments and changes also resonate with Kegan's and Marcia Baxter Magolda's idea of movement toward "self-authorship," or the internal capacity to define and coordinate one's beliefs, identity, and relationships (Baxter Magolda 2009; Kegan 1994). The gap year seems to have helped to catalyze movement toward self-authored ways of knowing, and it did so in many ways as it developed the interpersonal, intrapersonal, and cognitive capacities of the volunteers that underpin self-authorship.

One particular way the gap year experience seemed to catalyze development was by pushing volunteers toward a form of self-authorship almost by necessity—by "throwing [volunteers] into the deep end," as one described the gap year experience. In this light, the gap year might be viewed as a means of removing or at least suspending "privilege"—which Jane Pizzolato (2003) found to inhibit self-authorship—by placing volunteers into ambiguous situations in developing countries where there they were forced to make decisions of significance without clear pathways for success.

Thus, for instance, volunteers often realized that they could not ask their parents for help overseas when they were in trouble and that they had to "figure it out on [their] own." Volunteers also often encountered adversity and frustration—especially with their rate of cultural adaptation or their effectiveness as a volunteer—that prompted novel introspection. For instance, Brenda, who described her experience as "really challenging," said that the year "forced me to look at myself, to see myself for the first time." She captured her movement toward self-authorship as follows: "Before I was the person that my parents wanted me to be, but I realized I have my own personality and my own views. No one is pulling the strings anymore. You experience what you want to experience; you know who you are. You are in control of your own life."

Recognizing the shortcomings of relying on external formulas (ideas from others about what one should think and how one should act) about relationships, religion, morality, and identity led participants to enter a crossroads where their internal voices began to emerge. It also seems that these more self-authored ways of knowing are also cultivated before the gap year begins through the selection and fundraising process. In explaining to family, friends, and community members why they are fundraising—and in doing something somewhat countercultural, at least when volunteers come from a secondary school, family, or community without a significant tradition of international volunteering gap years—volunteers have to develop their own reasons and justifications for their gap year to others. Pizzolato (2003) found something similar in her study of high-risk students heading to college (e.g., students who were the first generation in their family to attend higher education). The process of developing their desires to attend college, and justifying to others why they wanted to do so, helped to catalyze more self-authored ways of thinking.

Developing self-authorship in the manner described by some of the gap year volunteers may raise particular difficulties. For instance, many of the volunteers struggled to integrate third-world perspectives with their situations back home, even years later. This suggests that Kegan's and Baxter Magolda's self-authorship and Mezirow's transformational learning may overstate the capabilities of agency of individuals—or at least not address the difficulties in developing and acting on our understandings of the world—to be an "author, maker, critic, and *re*-maker of its experience, the self as a system or complex, regulative of its parts" (Kegan 1994, 133). The experiences of gap year participants also illustrates the possible dangers in trying to push people to develop self-authorship under certain circumstances, as in the cases of those struggling with mental disorders.

This close examination of gap years also contributes to the literature on self-authorship by offering empirical evidence that may clarify and illustrate how what Pizzolato (2003) calls "provocative moments" can be externally induced by programs, such as an international volunteering gap year. These programs offer volunteers an opportunity to make repeated decisions in ambiguous situations, which may move young people toward self-authorship.

The Gap Year and Civic Meaning-making

So far, I have outlined how these volunteers' narratives suggest that the gap year contributed to the development of changes in their meaning-making—both their particular meanings that they make of themselves and the world around them (e.g., of religion, of their home country) and their more complex capacities for making meaning in the world (e.g., a more relative view of the world, greater self-authorship). As outlined in chapter 6, these changes in meaning-making can be given shape with the idea of *civic meaning-making*.

In chapter 6, we looked at how democratic and community participation rests on developmental foundations in interpersonal, intrapersonal, and cognitive dimensions, which together also comprise the underlying capacities necessary for self-authorship. Democratic citizens need the cognitive complexity to understand and assess multiple issues, the ability to engage and empathize with others' views and ways of being, and the intrapersonal understanding and identity development to maintain and express one's own voice amidst competing perspectives. Chapter 6 also sketched how Eyler and Giles's (1999) proposed elements of citizenship could be used as a framework for developing the concept of civic meaning-making. As I have cast them, these elements are: *values* (e.g., ideas of the good life and common good), *knowledge* (e.g., about social issues), *skills* (e.g., strategic knowledge about community affairs, interpersonal skills), *efficacy* (i.e., self-confidence), and *commitment* (e.g., desires and actions to help others and improve community life). Together, an expanded notion of these elements helped to illuminate the diverse and holistic capacities (intrapersonal, interpersonal, and cognitive), as well as the particular understandings and values that sustain an active democratic and community life.

Gap years contributed to growth in these dimensions. First, volunteers' narratives suggest that they cultivated their *capacities* for civic meaning-making. Interpersonally, volunteers expressed greater abilities to empathize and engage with others and to understand the effects of their actions on others. Intrapersonally, volunteers expressed a greater capacity to understand themselves and "control" how they experience reality. Further, their cognitive and problem-solving capacities increased; volunteers often described themselves as more "critical," "better," "more confident" decision-makers and students. Volunteers' narratives also reflect a greater awareness and ability to understand the complexity of social problems, the relative nature of the world, and the challenges in social and economic change, especially in the developing world.

In addition to these capacities, however, my research into gap years also suggests that the particular meanings that volunteers made shifted toward those that support democratic and community life. A more confident understanding of oneself was among the most prominent in the findings—many volunteers, even long after their gap year, discussed the heightened confidence the year away gave them, an element that affected several dimensions of their lives. Although many volunteers moved away from a more *idealistic* view of their potential impact on society, many also reported developing a more *efficacious* view of themselves, coupled with a more "realistic" (and often more limited) understanding of their potential impact.

Volunteers also seemed to develop an increased sense of connection to civic affairs, richer conceptions of the possibilities of community life, and a growing desire to take part in the world and contribute to others. This is especially important in light of evidence suggesting a decline in connectedness and community life in America and elsewhere (Putnam 2000). The volunteers' narratives reveal that the gap year is often an opportunity for volunteers to gain practical experience in community action, albeit in the developing world and at different levels depending on the volunteer's professional role in the community and the secondary projects in which the volunteer is engaged. Thus, the gap year seems to offer some volunteers experiences in deploying their civic meaning-making and acquiring skills as they are involved in forms of social change (e.g., setting up an education project) and working with community resources—resonating with the praxis or experiential emphasis that Paolo Freire emphasized in civic education (1970).

Much as Dewey argued in 1889 for the need to provide embryonic environments to develop the democratic dispositions and perspectives of young people, this study of the gap year suggests that the young volunteers were afforded a similar type of experience—especially as teachers and social care workers in small communities who had levels of responsibility, made decisions, and created secondary volunteering projects in their schools, organizations, and communities. They were participating and contributing to a community, and many felt it was the first time in their lives they had done so. Investing in the community seemed to have a reciprocal effect on volunteers: as they became more involved in the community, they felt more a part of it, and in turn made greater efforts for its sake. As one volunteer said: "I gave to the community, and I received a bunch back, so you feel grateful—connected—and you want to give more." As a result, volunteers often suggested that they had developed more positive and reciprocal conceptions of community as systems of mutual contribution among members. Ryan, a Uganda volunteer interviewed in his third year of college, offered an example of this: "It was really nice to know my neighbors overseas. . . . Before I was a citizen at the base level, but my year taught me more of what it meant to be a good citizen—that you have a responsibility to the people you are surrounded by." Thus, it seems that these gap years, especially when volunteers were placed in rural communities, acted to promote particular ways of making meaning of oneself and one's community, and thereby encouraged social behavior.

Although the actual impact of the volunteers' service to the gap year community may have been limited, their practical experience in civic engagement and newfound confidence seems to have prompted them to develop an understanding of themselves and of the world according to which they can—and should—make a positive contribution. Indeed, many continued to engage with volunteering and civic affairs, especially in the developing world—often attributing their motivations for these undertakings to their gap year experiences. As one volunteer in Peru put it: "The gap year is not about changing people's lives. . . . It's about realizing that you want to change other people's lives." Many volunteers brought these particular dispositions and ways of making meaning into alignment with their actions in college. Interviews with former volunteers indicated that they were continuing to work to make positive changes in society through research, advocacy, volunteering, and other means.

These narratives suggest the year helped to provide deeper purpose and meaning in volunteers' lives, a purpose grounded in others and a feeling of connection to something larger than themselves. This is especially important, because nearly a quarter of Americans now say they do not have a strong sense of what makes their lives meaningful—and because individuals with purpose and meaning are more fulfilled and more likely to support others in need (Baumeister et al. 2012). In this light, the idea of civic meaning-making helps to connect volunteers' understandings of the world with their deployment of these understandings in their actions after the year.

It seems that the gap years often acted as incubators of virtues, capacities, and perspectives needed in civic life. In other words, these international volunteering gap years helped to cultivate civic meaning-making.

Cosmopolitanism in Civic Meaning-making

So far we have seen how the international volunteering gap year seemed to promote civic meaning-making. This section examines the cosmopolitan dimension of this development in particular.

As outlined in chapter 6, this dimension of development can be understood by appeal to Martha Nussbaum's account of the three conditions for cosmopolitan thinking and action. These elements are: (1) "critical examination of oneself and one's tradition"; (2) ability of a person to see herself "not simply as a citizen of some local region or group but also and above all as a human being bound to all other human beings by ties, recognition and concern"; and (3) a narrative imagination, or the "ability to think what it might be like to be in the shoes of a person different from oneself, to be an intelligent reader of that person's story, and to understand the emotions and wishes and desires that someone so placed might have" (1997, 10–11). This section sketches how volunteers developed toward these meaning-making capacities and understandings of the world.

First, volunteers in this study often cited an increased ability and habit of criticizing and evaluating themselves, their home culture, and their way of being. One volunteer said that "as you learn about local culture you compare it to the UK and see differences, and people ask questions about UK culture and life, and you see the differences." Other volunteers discussed how they felt that the gap year helped them to become reflective about their own ways of being, as well as critical in their evaluations of the world.

Second, completing the gap year, and integrating into their community, helped volunteers evaluate and appreciate other ways of being. In so doing, it fostered a sense of connection to wider humanity and an appreciation of the relevant differences and commonalities among peoples. Kara, a volunteer in Chile, offered this perspective: "I have gained a respect for other people, being friendly and interested in other people no matter ethnicity, race, color or beliefs." Another volunteer said that he realized the commonalties amongst peoples during his year and that we are "all human beings." Acting on this, volunteers often expressed criticism of others' bias or lack of intercultural understanding—especially the media, public organizations, peer groups, and international charity communities. In addition, volunteers became more involved in international affairs through their peer groups in college (e.g., international student groups), as well as in greater advocacy, campaigning, research, and volunteering on global issues after their return.

Third, volunteers often experienced a greater ability to understand the world—to "personalize the developing world," as one put it—and a greater ability to tolerate differences and empathize with others both locally and internationally. This suggests the development of greater narrative imagination in Nussbaum's sense. Volunteers also developed a more relative understanding of the world, which enabled them to better evaluate and understand moral practices and ways of being in a contextual light. Furthermore, they often developed a certain depth to their understanding of their gap year country's culture, a depth that helped them recognize their own ignorance of much of the world, which they attributed to the duration and immersion of the yearlong experience.

Summary

In the previous two chapters, I outlined a theoretical framework of learning and meaning-making. In this chapter, I showed how the gap year participants' experiences fit into that framework.

The concept of meaning-making—with integrated roots in transformational learning and constructive-developmental perspectives—proved helpful in developing a lens to "make meaning" of the volunteers' narratives. By connecting the literature on citizenship formation with the developmental and transformational learning literatures, we arrived at the distinctive construct of civic meaning-making. This construct helps to integrate often separate fields and thereby contributes to each in significant ways.

Further, the framework developed for this study of gap year experiences responds to calls for greater research in student development and learning using a more holistic or integrated approach. As King and Baxter Magolda (1996, 163–164) have asserted, "A successful educational experience simultaneously increases cognitive understanding, a sense of personal maturity, and interpersonal effectiveness." My research indicates that the international volunteering gap year may help development in each of these areas.

According to Baxter Magolda, universities too readily supply students with formulas for success, so they do not have to develop self-authored ways of knowing (2001). Although I did not look at a comparative sample in creating this study, we can draw the tentative conclusion that the gap year offers such opportunities for developing more complex meaning-making schemes, which also underpin the concept of self-authorship. One particular way the gap year experience seemed to catalyze development was by pushing volunteers toward a form of self-authorship almost by necessity.

As a foundational study of the international volunteering gap year, this research has highlighted some key areas of change that volunteers reported from their experiences. As Shkedi maintains, a theory premised on qualitative evidence is put forward "not as a universal truth but as a theoretical rationale for the particular phenomenon under investigation" (2004, 632). In other words, it is constructed in the context of particular students and thus describes possibilities rather than generalizable descriptions (Baxter Magolda 2008).

I hope this book provides fertile ground for further investigation into the changes that volunteers undergo when they undertake an international volunteer gap year. In so doing, it will contribute to the debate about the possible impacts of an international volunteering gap year. As I discuss further in the next chapter, this book presents future researchers of the gap year with clear areas to investigate with greater detail or different data collection instruments, such as the changes in civic perceptions of volunteers.

The next chapter, concerning designing the gap year, is largely practitioner-oriented. But it also makes a theoretical contribution by further developing ideas about the mechanisms through which changes in meaning-making can be facilitated. It builds on the book thus far and explores, using lessons and reports from volunteers' experiences, some of the programmatic elements in the gap year that may encourage or hinder this type of learning and development.

8

Designing Gap Year Programs

All gap years are not equally educational. But when we examine the programmatic influences on volunteers' experiences, we can begin to see how the gap year can be constructed as a pedagogical tool. We can attempt to design the gap year to maximize learning for participants, while respecting the culture and aspirations of developing communities around the world.

The Limits of a Pedagogy

Before beginning a discussion on such a design, it is important to first acknowledge the limits of a possible pedagogy for the gap year. In an effort to maximize learning or safety, gap year program administrators may have a desire to control the experience or, as Kate Simpson (2004) advocates, to include a greater formal, didactic component into the gap year, much like service-learning courses in the United States. From the diversity of motivations, experiences, and changes volunteers expressed in their narratives, it becomes increasingly clear that there is often only so much a gap year administrator can control or insert in gap years and still have a "gap year" program. Indeed, people are attracted to the idea of a gap year often because it is a year *out* of formal education, a year of difference, immersion, and risk where one is granted a degree of freedom and autonomy typically not permitted in formal educational environments. Imposing such control may detract potential volunteers, restrict volunteer exploration and development of independent projects, and reduce the challenges and dissonance during the year—which seem to be central to learning in the experience.

To be sure, program administrators can play important roles for gap year students beyond providing safe overseas placements and logistical support. Providers can do a great deal to provide substantive training to students before departure (e.g., in mental health, cultural and political dynamics, volunteering roles, what to expect overseas, work and personal life balance). They can provide students with intellectual scaffolding and guided reflection as they wrestle with changing ideas about the world and their role within it and encouragement to engage with a variety of activities during volunteers' time overseas. These opportunities for program administrators will be discussed in more detail below.

A Pedagogy

Even in the face of limitations on the design and pedagogy, administrators can play an influential role in helping to create an educationally powerful environment for volunteers. Overall, the central aim is to find or create a placement and environment that provides an optimal balance between challenge and support for volunteers. The way of living and work roles should be sufficiently different from their previous lives, sustained, and challenging to stimulate productive dissonance and renegotiation of ways of understanding the world. In essence, as a pedagogical tool, the gap year aims to catalyze the development of more complex meaning-making capabilities and changes in particular made meanings. This process can lead volunteers to a greater understanding of themselves and the world with stronger intrapersonal, interpersonal, and cognitive foundations. In many ways, the gap year is an integrative pedagogy that targets the heart, mind, and soul of volunteers, something Parker Palmer (2010) believes is central to "transformative" education that changes the way people think, feel, and act.

Often, the specific avenues toward creating this environment aim for greater integration and involvement in the community for volunteers; as one said: "I changed because I lived as a local." The primary catalyst for change within gap year participants was often an intense and long-term engagement with multiple forms of difference, and efforts toward immersion can be a reflection of this type of engagement. The literature on higher education can help capture this idea. Alexander Astin's theory of student involvement posits that the "quality and quantity of the student's academic and personal development is a direct function of the student's degree of involvement" (1984, 297). Astin defines involvement as the "amount of time and physical and psychological energy that the student devotes to the learning experience" (1984, 297). The effectiveness of a gap year as a pedagogical instrument appears to consist of, in part, a combination of several forms of involvement (e.g., acculturation into a very different culture, relationships, and demanding volunteering roles) that capture the energy, reflection, and interactions of volunteers.

Overall, it is important to emphasize that each student engages with the gap year in his or her own unique way and at different intensities. As a period of relative autonomy and flexibility, the gap year provides a space for a wide breadth of interests to be explored at varying depths by the student. Below, I sketch some of the key programmatic variables that seem to influence the learning and the changes reported by volunteers during their international volunteering gap year. These form the more specific elements of an emerging pedagogy and design for the gap year.

Variables

Challenge

As stated above, finding a gap year placement and environment that provides an optimal challenge for volunteers is critical to the learning process. The belief about the connection between challenge and learning rests on a view of learning that posits that it principally happens from the "challenge of new experiences and information to the way things are believed to be. Growth rests on puzzlement, on challenge to current perspectives, and on the challenge to resolve the conflict. Students develop more complex and adequate ways of viewing the world when they are challenged not overwhelmed by new experiences" (Eyler and Giles, 184–185).

The challenge for gap year administrators is thus to match the desires and personal development potential of the volunteer to the optimal level of challenge and support in a project, which can be ascertained to some extent when selecting participants. A range of placements could be offered to match the desires and perceived abilities of volunteers. For instance, one volunteer said he wanted a highly challenging project and was sent to work on the streets of Bolivia with troubled youth; another was sent to an extremely isolated and rural project in Namibia, and one was sent to an isolated aboriginal village in the rain forest in Guyana. On the other end, one volunteer who wanted a project that was not that difficult and challenging was sent to Santiago, Chile, where he felt the culture, work, and life were not as demanding as other projects. A range of levels of support and on-site staff can also be offered to accommodate students' needs and ease worries of potential gap year students and their families.

Anecdotally, however, it seemed that volunteers who were in a culture and work role that were most different from their previous lives—which most challenged the way they made meaning—reported some of the greatest changes in the year. One volunteer who worked in a rural school in Honduras said her year was "more challenging than fun" and that "you need to have those times when you just want to pack your bags and want to leave; you learn so much; you grow more if you have that challenge." Tom, a volunteer in South Africa, said: "I think that our project threw us in the deep end. There was little help from our colleagues. . . . However, it was a really good experience to be not helped and have to work it out for ourselves and to have the level of responsibility that we were given." In addition, many volunteers said they were the most fulfilled or enjoyed the year when they overcame great challenges. Gregory, a volunteer in China, said: "The greatest enjoyment came from the hardest challenges."

Sometimes, though, there was a mismatch between challenge level and the volunteer. Finding the "optimal challenge" for volunteers is difficult—sometimes the project is too challenging for the volunteers and they depart early, but sometimes the project is not challenging enough, and the volunteer leaves early or becomes disillusioned and does not feel needed and appreciated. For instance, volunteers in Santiago, Chile, a place where a gap year provider organization staff said sometimes less motivated and more introverted volunteers are sent, reported that the year was not as challenging as it could have been for them, and they felt they would have gained more if it was. Tobias, for example, summed up the year saying that "I wanted something that was easier than the other gap year projects, but maybe that was too easy." In either case, volunteers may leave feeling that they did not get their "maximum benefit" out of their year. However, it seems that a careful selection and volunteer placement process can help mediate this, which I discuss further in the next section.

Despite efforts of gap year administrators, unexpected events and situations overseas can occur that are incredibly challenging for volunteers and require greater overseas support by staff members and the local community. As discussed in chapter 5, volunteers can be presented with significant events, such as the death of a child in their care, or be given too much responsibility, which can be potentially harmful. In some cases, volunteers sought psychological counseling after their year. One gap year organization staff member highlighted this:

> The kids who go in there, get the job done and don't take it home with them at night, often do much better in the social projects because they don't take on the emotional fragility and the vulnerability of the kids that they are working with. And that is something that you have to be careful of. You are working with bright,

beautiful, creative individuals, and you don't want empty shells coming home . . . we actively encourage them to take a couple of weeks holiday at the end, because coming day after day after day in the care home and then come back is just such a shock to the system so they need to get that break.

The director of one gap year provider noted that exposure to suffering and traumatic events during their year can potentially be harmful for the volunteers' emotional and mental health. Thus, psychological support services to process experiences and encouragement from staff to take vacations seems warranted.

Country and Project Community Selection

The selection of the country and the community can be important elements in thinking about this challenge for volunteers. The central benefit of a gap year placement in a developing country seems to be the productive dissonance (see chapter 6) that these settings can provide. It is unlikely that a person would have her assumptions about herself and the world around her challenged with the same intensity, frequency, and breadth if she stayed in the developed world. Going overseas also helps to cultivate a type of independence and self-confidence that staying close to home in a familiar cultural environment probably would not. In addition, the unique more rural or at least unfamiliar settings of the gap year can often stimulate specific perspectives in volunteers that we need more of in the world. A gap year in a developing community may help foster, for example, a conception of community that is more active and intimate—an outcome that may be unlikely in many study abroad settings in larger cities (for more on urban versus rural settings, see below).

Developing countries also allow young people to have access to roles for which they probably would not be eligible candidates in the developed world (such as an English teacher) because of professional barriers. Granted, this leads to much criticism of international volunteers and their impact on local communities, as mentioned in the introductory chapter. Of course, these volunteers may not be as skilled or as highly trained as their older counterparts (such as physicians with Doctors Without Borders). But these eager young people do have some skills (such as being a native English speaker) and perspectives that are interesting and potentially helpful—especially with some training and professional support. Balancing a volunteer's desire to help, his or her training, and the needs of the local community can be difficult, and we *should* critically evaluate the developmental contributions of gap year placements in communities. That

said, it is important to remember that these gap year placements are not principally designed to be international development projects—they are largely educational endeavors for the volunteers. These educational experiences can then
provide a source of motivation and intimate knowledge so that participants can
make contributions to the developing world and elsewhere in public service
throughout their lives. As mentioned in chapter 5, it is not uncommon for people who undertook a gap year to be in roles in international development or
other public service later in life.

However, these claims about the value of these international volunteering
gap years do not intend to discount the educational value of formal study abroad
or domestic gap year programs, such as the organization City Year in the United
States, which offers volunteers ages 17–24 yearlong placements with high-need
schools in America. These domestic settings can offer different points of reflection for the volunteer than do international settings, such as the particular barriers to changing educational practices within an American educational institution. Regardless of the location of the year, providers should consider the local
context and the various tools and opportunities they have to engage students
with difference in a particular setting.

As a general principle, international gap year administrators should consider
each volunteer's capabilities and a country's culture. The culture should be sufficiently different so that it challenges, in many ways, volunteers' understandings and perspectives of their ways of being. One volunteer illustrated how this
happened for her:

> Until you go overseas I think one's imagination has a huge part in how one en-
> visages things in the world . . . living there allowed their customs to seep into my
> way of living. I only really understood how much my outlook had changed when
> I came home; I found myself looking at everything like an outsider, questioning
> and philosophizing the same way as when I had first arrived in the Dominican
> Republic. Perhaps what I am trying to say is that questioning the way we live is
> only possible when you know what you want to ask, and that really can only
> come when you have seen a different way of living.

A volunteer in Honduras experienced a similar effect: "On a deeper level I
learnt a lot of lessons and things that I had never thought about before because
I used to take life in the West for granted. This year helped me start to question
further things I had only begun to think about before I went away."

Sometimes, volunteers reported that they thought their gap year country was not "different enough" and that they would have learned more had it been so. One volunteer in Santiago, Chile, said: "I left London and it wasn't that different when I arrived in Santiago. Chile embraced Western ideals—it was surprising because how similar it is—I didn't learn a lot about a different culture; I learned a lot about the culture I just left. I wanted something more different." In these settings that have fewer cultural differences, it is important to encourage volunteers to look deeper in the culture and seek to understand a more nuanced view.

Another factor to consider when selecting a project country is its receptivity; a community can be more hospitable to cultural differences or more demanding of volunteers. As an example of this, one provider staff member staff posited that in Thailand the "hosts are less demanding and the culture demands less of the volunteers. They don't verbalize and say you're not doing a good job there, plus they are used to tourists more. In the past, it was a place that we sent weaker volunteers, but that can be bad because it is cheap and easy to party, so you have to have control." After learning about the projects in Uganda from other former volunteers, one participant who spent his year in Thailand said: "Their projects seemed harder, more challenging . . . maybe we would have gained more if it was more challenging." However, living and acting in a culture and community that seems to be receptive to visitors' cultural mistakes, such as Thailand, can facilitate learning too. One volunteer in Thailand remarked: "It is easier to put yourself out there. They think it is fine if you do wrong; you're not used to the culture."

In addition, since volunteers often learned from local perspectives on issues, such as marriage in India, and sometimes adopted elements of these perspectives in their lives after the gap year, it might be helpful to think about the types of changes one wants to promote in volunteers. If one wanted a volunteer to develop a more critical perspective of the media, for instance, sending a volunteer to China seems to be a way to encourage this. Similarly, if one wanted to encourage volunteers to develop an awareness and appreciation of different forms and roles of family, a community with a strong emphasis on family might be a more helpful placement.

Integration

At the same time, finding placements that will allow volunteers to integrate into their community seems important to the learning process. Integration encourages encountering and living different ways of being at greater frequency and with greater depth, as Paul, a South African volunteer put it: "To understand the culture, you have to see it from the inside; otherwise you wouldn't be able to get people's personal insights. And as you compare your values to other people you realize that your values aren't as infallible as you once thought." Likewise, Ryan, a volunteer in Uganda, said: "To integrate is to change the way you see things— after, you're not so rigid in your thoughts."

Several programmatic variables seem to influence integration. One should consider the merits of an urban placement to a rural one. People in rural settings often seemed—and reported—to be more integrated in their wider communities and culture than those in urban placements. For instance, one volunteer who lived in an aboriginal village in the rain forest of Guyana said that he changed over his year, because he "lived as local" and was able to see the world from a "villager's perspective." In fact, he said that he was so integrated that he could have "found a wife" and lived there.

Urban placements may limit the integration of volunteers into the wider community. Urban settings often suggest that there are more Western stores and people, greater technology to communicate back to the West, more English speakers, and less pressure to be involved in the life of the community. Tobias, a volunteer in Santiago, Chile, explained that in cities there is "pressure" to remain "anonymous" and "not take an interest in others' lives." Tobias said that he wanted to be "forced" to develop relationships with local people to become more extroverted, but that his urban placement did not do this for him and that Santiago was not "different enough" from his home in London. After visiting his peers in rural projects and seeing them after they returned, he said: "I think the people in rural villages got more out of it." One volunteer even went as far as to say that she felt gap year volunteers should only be sent to rural communities. This was a sentiment echoed by some other volunteers in large cities, who were "disappointed" that their project was not very different from their home country or that they didn't have the same "opportunities to get involved" as their peers in more rural locations. As discussed earlier in chapter 4, social science research supports volunteers' observations that there may be more opportunities and expectations for social and civic involvement in rural communities. Robert Putnam (2000), for instance, found that metropolitan environments tend to have weaker social capital and less civic engagement than do smaller towns. Residents in metropolitan areas are significantly less likely to attend public meetings, to be active in community organizations, visit friends, or work on community projects (Putnam 2000).

Relationships with local people, which volunteers routinely said were critical to learning, can also sometimes be easier to form in rural communities. Often, insights and new understanding of a culture were facilitated by personal relationships with local people developed over the course of the year, as seen in chapter 3. Furthermore, relationships were critical to building the emotional connection to the people and issues in the country, as well as providing a support group that often helped motivate volunteers to stay involved in their gap year country or give back locally and internationally after their gap year.

Whether a volunteer is in an urban or rural placement also seems to influence the sense of community volunteers developed overseas. In considering urban and rural placements, administrators may consider the level of involvement a volunteer could have with various activities in the community over their year and the sense of community that one may want to try to develop an appreciation for in the volunteer. More active and intimate senses of community were often found among volunteers in rural placements.

However, the close-knit rural communities can also be difficult for volunteers to adjust to, as volunteers are often the subject of gossip and have only infrequent experiences outside the same small community. As a result, one volunteer said she sometimes felt "claustrophobic" in her rural, small community, and another said she felt "naked" with the constant attention that her arrival into the community brought.

Although there might be a greater diversity of activities, such as art groups or different social groups in urban settings, counterintuitively, it might be easier to be involved in a diversity of activities in rural communities. It may be more difficult to find these activities in urban placements, and there might be greater barriers to entry. For instance, a volunteer in rural placement in southern Chile became a firefighter during her year, but it seems unlikely—and perhaps unwise—that she could have become one in Santiago, Chile.

Further, a city location may increase the expectations volunteers have of availability of support during the year, whereas volunteers in more isolated, developing communities may not have the same expectations of support (due to practical limitations) and be more encouraged to resolve problems and issues on their own. All this said, urban environments can certainly be highly educational placements that engage students with difference and offer points of reflection and opportunities that rural locations may not. Regardless of the setting, gap year administrators should encourage students to take advantage of the local context and opportunities to take part in new and different activities.

Location of Volunteer Accommodations

A gap year administrator may also want to consider the location of accommodations for the volunteers, which seems to influence the engagement with the culture and integration during the year. There are drawbacks and advantages to different types. For example, having a volunteer live with a local family may provide an immersion into the language and culture more—as well as more support for the volunteer—but it may also limit the freedom and autonomy of volunteers over their year. Having volunteers live where they work, such as in an orphanage, may provide constant interaction with some elements of local culture and people, but, with little respite from work, the year can also be especially stressful. Volunteers may then burn out and want to leave early. Finally, having volunteers live in their own house or apartment may encourage independence, but it may also limit the engagement volunteers have in the local culture or community.

Diverse Social Networks

Furthermore, it seems important that volunteers have a diverse social network during their year, and administrators may consider the opportunities for volunteers to engage with people of a broad variety of ages, backgrounds, and roles in selecting projects. As discussed in chapter 3, having diverse social networks has been shown in universities to help develop cognitive and moral capacities in young people (Derryberry and Thoma 2000), and the gap year environment can provide—and encourage—this type of broad interaction.

For example, in her debriefing session from her year in rural Chile, Paulina discussed how interacting and developing relationships with people of all ages benefitted her, reflecting that before her year, "I was always around the same people, and people my age, it just wasn't developing me." Similarly, a volunteer reported that "I came back and my friends at home . . . they were all the same and hadn't changed. In my year, I was in a new community and changing, and that made me see how my home and community had formed me."

Separation from Previous Environment

In encouraging both integration in the gap year community and independence, it seems important that volunteers are permitted and encouraged to live largely removed from their previous lives in their home countries. Many volunteers in this study felt that living removed from the social pressures of their home country was "liberating" for them and allowed them to act with a freedom that they did not have in to the same degree in their home countries.

Separating from a previous environment often means that volunteers should limit the communication they have with their life back home, including their parents and friends. In this study, limiting engagement with one's hometown often encouraged volunteers to make local friends, aided in language acquisition, and encouraged independence. Reflecting this, one volunteer recalled: "You often need help over there, but there is no one there—you just have to figure it out. Before I would have called my parents or friends to help, but there you can't—you just have to figure it out." Access to the Internet may also inhibit integration into the local culture if used excessively, providing what some volunteers described as an "escape." Tobias, a volunteer in Santiago, Chile, reported playing multiplayer Internet games on the computer when he arrived on his year, something that limited his interactions with the local culture. He recalled that early in his year "I sat inside on my computer in the UK, and I did the same thing a lot in Santiago."

Sending volunteers in large country groups where they are in project sites near each other (and thus can meet as a group often) can also inhibit integration and language learning. Furthermore, as some participants suggested, large groups of foreign volunteers can make local people feel intimidated and not as likely to approach and befriend volunteers. In fact, volunteers whose partners left during the year said that their relationships with local people became the strongest afterward. Having no partner forced them to become more integrated and to speak more of the local language. Thus, sending volunteers with very limited numbers of partners (i.e., one partner or even no partner) seems to encourage integration.

Project and Work Role Selection

Providing participants with volunteering roles of genuine responsibility in the community, where they could make a difference in the life of another, can be important for the volunteer. This responsibility can encourage participants to invest in the year, develop a curiosity about the culture that is often grounded in real world problems, and stay throughout the entire gap year. In fact, despite largely egoistic motivations before the year, this study found that volunteers' motivations often became more altruistic during the course of the year. In addition, the feeling that one is a role model in one's work also seemed to influence volunteers' behavior and encourage introspection. Occupying an adult role, or being perceived as an adult, seems to influence volunteers' self-concept. One provider organization recognizes this and refers to and tries to treat its volunteers as adults. The relationship between providing roles of responsibility and increased learning has been documented by Janet Eyler and Dwight Giles (1999) in their study of service learning in the United States. These professional roles can provide a context for young people to take leadership roles, act resourcefully and creatively, and see how their skills can make a difference, which can contribute to higher self-confidence and self-efficacy (Eyler and Giles 1999). Specifically, having high levels of responsibility where their performance affected others seemed to encourage volunteers in this study to work hard and give themselves more to the project. These opportunities for responsibility often allowed volunteers to successfully accomplish tasks in their year and acquire more skills as they became more confident. As one said: "I gained the most from situations where I was given a lot of responsibility."

The specific type of work that volunteers have also seems to influence the integration into the wider community. For instance, teachers, especially in rural communities, often reported high levels of integration in the community, especially with local families of the children they were teaching. In contrast, narratives from volunteers who lived and worked in orphanages suggest they sometimes experienced less integration into their larger community, stating that the orphanage was their community.

In a related concept, within one provider organization, there is a common saying that a "busy volunteer is a happy volunteer," illustrating that the level of activity (often within their work role) is associated with the enjoyment and fulfillment of volunteers and should be considered in project selection. When advising local organizations that host volunteers overseas, one provider suggests that volunteers who have a "heavy work load feel needed and appreciated. Those who have too light a workload can become disillusioned." This was reflected in this study. As an example of this, one returned volunteer who worked at an orphanage said that she had a "bad year" relative to her peers because "I wasn't busy enough—I would just sit around when kids were at school." She said she "didn't feel connected to the community" since she stayed in the orphanage.

Secondary Projects

Developing secondary projects (those that volunteers create over the year to address a local issue, such as working with a sports team or tutoring), seems to influence volunteers in a number of ways, including integration in the local community and development of their sense of confidence, efficacy, and community. Facilitating opportunities for volunteers to find and develop secondary projects can therefore help them invest in the year in new ways and benefit as a result.

However, certain placements may not accommodate secondary projects. For instance, one volunteer who worked in an orphanage said: "Apart from some classes during the summer holidays, we didn't manage to set up any secondary projects, as the Aldea has a very strict timetable for the children and we were not permitted to organize timetabled activities." Although there is an element of personal responsibility and volunteer agency in seeking new endeavors and secondary projects, finding placements that allow for other activities as well as encouraging volunteers to find these opportunities seems helpful.

Selection of Volunteers

Given the lack of low-income students who have historically taken a gap year, program administrators should make a considerable effort to recruit students from low-income areas. We need people from all socioeconomic backgrounds to have the opportunity to receive the education a gap year can provide. Recruiting more low-income students may be challenging for a number of reasons, but offering examples of how this investment paid off for other students may be one approach. A more diverse population may also have need special and different support when overseas.

When selecting volunteers, gap year administrators need to consider not only how the volunteer may benefit from the year, but the potential benefit a volunteer can offer to a gap year community. A potential volunteer who has behavioral problems, for instance, may not be a suitable candidate and could potentially harm the local community or at the very least provide a distraction rather than needed support. Administrators may also consider how the personality and characteristics of the volunteers will interact with a particular volunteering role and culture.

Furthermore, despite the potential for developmental gains with candidates that have mental health disorders, caution is warranted when selecting these volunteers. Giving special attention to screening potential volunteers for mental health disorders seems necessary, especially since the stress and pressures of the gap year can trigger a resurgence of a mental health disorder. Mental health problems can also go unnoticed or untreated overseas in communities without adequate mental health infrastructure. Volunteers' mental health challenges can also lead to early departures from a gap year experience. Although volunteers can certainly benefit from a shortened gap year, leaving early can potentially be a negative experience for both the host organization and the volunteer. Selecting suitable candidates for the year also has consequences for the gap year organization; unstable volunteers can damage the reputation of the organization in the local community and limit possibilities for future volunteer placements. Also, with current concerns about violence and people with certain mental illnesses, screening for serious mental disorders seems prudent.

Encouraging Volunteer Reflection

Although some volunteers certainly come to the gap year experience with habits of substantive reflection and inquisitiveness, there are a number of ways that organizations can attempt to encourage reflection and provide intellectual scaffolding for participants. In many respects, gap year providers can learn from the service-learning courses popular in universities in the United States, and administrators could look to examples from these courses for suggestions to enhance learning during a gap year.

Kate Simpson (2004) is critical of gap year provider organizations for not providing greater didactic elements in their programs and for the lack of academic and pedagogical resources to participants. She argues that provider organizations rely on experience alone for volunteers' education, and she believes that this leads to simplistic and crude understandings of the developing world. While some didactic component seems helpful, this empirical research illustrates how even with limited didactic components and educational resources, a structured, long-term placement, which encourages integration, can help volunteers develop more sophisticated understandings of international development and culture. Moreover, as this research has shown, learning about the culture and international development is important, but is not the only way in which volunteers grow during the year. Volunteers can benefit in diverse ways from partner relationships, independence, and teaching roles, to name a few. A more holistic and broad conception of learning will help researchers and program administrators appreciate and plan for the diversity of ways in which volunteers are influenced by different gap year experiences.

There are, however, a number of strategies organizations can employ to help facilitate greater cultural understanding and volunteer reflection. First, an ethos of curiosity and critical analysis of the world within the organization can help cultivate an interest in understanding the culture of each country. During volunteer training, administrators can begin to discuss the dynamics of the gap year country's culture, economy, history, and politics. Providers can offer a recommended reading list of books and articles or a list of useful websites on their gap year countries, and each country's society can be discussed with volunteers there. Reading and exploring each country and region in training, even if briefly, may help give a foundation of understanding and begin a habit of critical analysis and inquisitiveness that the volunteer can build on during the year. Further, organizations can engage future volunteers with debates around the ethics and efficacy of international development, challenging students' assumptions about the contributions they may make in their developing community.

Gap year provider organizations can attempt to cultivate further curiosity over the year by encouraging volunteers to be critical and question what is around them and how it is operating, providing news articles, and requesting and supporting students as they produce reports or research projects on particular aspects of the community or culture. However, it is largely up to the volunteer's own curiosity to sustain an active and critical analysis of the culture and issues before them. Gap years are flexible and present volunteers with an array of issues that they can attempt to understand and in which they can become involved. Indeed, volunteers often become engaged with particular aspects of the country that reflect their own interest, such as the political elections or the language and its history. As outlined throughout this chapter, placing volunteers in positions of real responsibly in the community and facilitating integration can help foster this level of curiosity and learning.

Simpson's call for a more explicit educational component must also be balanced with volunteers' desire for a break from formal education, a central motivator of young people in taking gap years in the first place. Requiring more academic assignments may detract from the gap year's popularity among young people. That said, gap year organizations can encourage reflection by asking participants to journal, blog, or respond to particular prompts about their perspectives and current events. These need not restrict volunteer autonomy; volunteers can use these as tools to monitor their thinking and process their experiences. Staff from community partners or the gap year organization can also discuss their experiences and changing thoughts with volunteers, serving as co-learners, cultural informants, mentors, and facilitators to catalyze student reflection and learning during the gap year.

The learning and reflection on the gap year can continue after volunteers return home, and a debriefing and reflection session for volunteers can be helpful. This session can help students discuss their year with other volunteers and place their experiences in context with other countries or volunteer placements. It can also be provide time for counseling and guidance for future plans, as well as help volunteers after their year find resources to help them process their experiences after coming home. In addition, the session can be used to help volunteers think about the ways they can build upon the skills and perspectives they have gained during their gap year in college and beyond. Volunteers could also be encouraged to use their time in higher education as a period to reflect further on their experiences, using the academic resources to place their year within more formal theoretical contexts, and to take action on the perspectives and values that volunteers may have developed over the year.

Fundraising

Given the lack of low-income students who take gap years or volunteer internationally, assisting students with fundraising is especially important if the practice is to expand to a greater range of the population. With the relatively lower cost of a gap year compared with traditional study abroad, with enough time, students can often fundraise the entire cost of a gap year. Gap year students employ a variety of techniques to garner donations, and fundraising assistance websites (i.e., crowdfunding platforms) make it easier for them to communicate their message and receive money from family, friends, community organizations, and charitable groups. In the future, a greater number of universities may also be able to assist students with funding for a gap year.

In addition to the monetary assistance that fundraising provides, it seems that having volunteers fundraise for their gap year can provide other benefits. Volunteers often cited that fundraising helped them prepare for the experience, gave them a greater investment in the year, and built more confidence before heading overseas. Furthermore, fundraising provided motivation for volunteers to stay through the year, because they did not want to embarrass themselves or discredit the donors by coming back early. Volunteers also suggested that fundraising helped them feel that the year as a whole was a personal accomplishment, which, in turn, built confidence.

Training

Training for volunteers seems essential, especially for those right out of high school, who may face particular challenges overseas without their families and who are often travelling abroad for the first time. Training can be a time for education about the risks and safety concerns with living overseas, as well as discussion about the ethics and efficacy of international volunteers, local cultures, and current events in each gap year country. Moreover, training, especially with volunteers who will be teachers and social care workers, can help them to be more effective in their placements during the year. Training can also be useful in providing advice on how to balance work with personal life to avoid burnout, as well as how to form bonds between volunteers before departing.

Length

Administrators and students should also consider the length of a gap year program. Longer-term placements, lasting eight to twelve months, can often make it easier to place students overseas because they can be, for example, a teacher for an entire academic year. It also takes time to integrate into the local culture and learn about a country, especially to experience the different seasons of the year. Longer-term placements helped the volunteers in this study to integrate in the local community, understand the culture, and learn the language. Living a different way of life for a longer period can also help shape volunteers' desires for certain ways of living, such as a desire for a specific type of community. Shorter-term placements, or those of just a few weeks or few months, limit the learning and personal development of a gap year.

Volunteers in this study nearly universally advocated for an entire year experience. One volunteer argued how a long-term placement can influence one's orientation and disposition during the year: "You need to stay there for year. If you are going to be there for 12 months you have to invest yourself—you have to build friendships and relationships. If you're there for the short term you can just keep your mind thinking about your home country and not really invest in the community—and before you know it—you're gone." Volunteers also illustrated how the last few months of their year were especially beneficial for them. As one volunteer said: "After 10 months, I learned to see the world from a completely different point of view from the one I grew up with." Another volunteer in Uganda reported: "I thought I knew the country after 6 months, then at 8 months I realized that I still didn't know the culture. It was only when I was leaving did I feel that I was finally getting a grasp of what was going on." Advocating for a full year program, one volunteer who spent her time abroad in the Dominican Republic expressed:

> A full year feels so complete, like a whole chapter. It feels much more whole, a bite rather than a nibble . . . my last 4 months were my best months . . . it took that long to really know the country and build the relationships, but it felt complete . . . There is something to be said for staying for all the seasons; you see fruit in winter and have outside activities and in the summer more indoor activities. When I was leaving, the same fruit as when I arrived came again and the weather began to change—it felt complete—that I was leaving the same place that I had come to.

Longer-term placements also increase the chances that the volunteer may make a contribution to the gap year community. As one returned volunteer shared: "It takes more than a few months to learn how to teach." Often, volunteers felt that the last few months of their gap year was the time they finally felt comfortable and useful in their project, something that helped to develop their confidence and feelings of efficacy. Jeffrey highlighted this: "The last four months was when I felt completely useful and happy in my project. I enjoyed witnessing the results of my own hard work and of others." Further, secondary projects were typically established by volunteers in the latter half of the year, after the volunteer felt he or she understood the community and its problems—and was comfortable enough—to act in a new setting. As mentioned in the section above, secondary projects can help volunteers feel involved and develop their sense of confidence and self-efficacy.

Finally, the longer-term experience allowed for volunteers to travel during their year, experience more places and people, and return to their home country to start a new academic year without much delay. A gap year provider staff member outlined a benefit of a quick return to college: "If they were to come home in May they have got three months; they have done a nine month placement . . . their friends are off at university and getting on with their own things and you have got this treading water stage, and I think that can be quite destructive."

Volunteer Partners

Gap year volunteers are often paired with one (or two) other volunteers for their year. These partnerships can influence the learning experience of the gap year, and attention to this is warranted when placing and supporting volunteers.

Partnerships have the potential to develop into very close relationships, which provide mutual support to persevere, reflect, and develop interpersonally.

Typically paired with same sex partners, volunteers often reported developing very close relationships with their partners; however, not all partnerships matured like this. Volunteers were sometimes more like acquaintances or had difficulties getting along. Moreover, matching a volunteer with a seemingly complementary partner, such as placing a confident volunteer with relatively shy volunteer, can help with integration and the overall experience. However, partnership pairing is often unpredictable—and these distinct characteristics may cause tension in their relationships.

Timing

It seems that taking a gap year before college (as opposed to later in life) can have particular benefits. By taking a gap year at an early point in one's life, one has more time to capitalize on the learning and development that may occur. As this study found, completing the gap year helped participants cultivate a variety of skills and capabilities that they believed helped them take more advantage of their college experience. Many volunteers, for instance, felt the gap year helped them determine their vocation and made them "better students." Economic research from Australia on students who took a gap year supports this assertion. Elisa Birch and Paul Miller (2007) found a "significant positive impact" on gap year students' academic performance in college, with the strongest impact for those who had applied to college with grades on the lower end of the distribution.

In addition, the gap year provided caretaking roles that, particularly for male volunteers, they may not have otherwise had. Volunteers suggested that these roles expanded their capacities for empathy and patience. Developing these qualities as a young person may help him or her to have more flourishing and fulfilling experiences for a greater part of his or her life.

Finally, brain research suggests that when people are young, their brains are more malleable and they more able to learn and change (Pujol et al. 1993). Brain research also suggests that many regions of the brain are not developed until the twenties and that being in an environment that is hyper-stimulating might be helpful for long-term brain functioning (Pujol et al. 1993). Gap years may provide such an environment. That said, the brain is adaptable and learning can happen over the life course, so taking a gap year could be beneficial at any point in one's life.

Where to Next?

I hope that this holistic study provides a foundation upon which future studies in the emerging field of gap year research can build. Some elements future studies could include could be comparing programs in different countries or with different demographics, using a more longitudinal design, and having a more focused analysis of particular programmatic variables and volunteer learning.

In this study, I attempted to better integrate the fields of constructive-developmental theory, transformational learning, and civic education, but future work is needed to continue and refine these efforts. Further research could particularly examine the idea of civic meaning-making, as well as the usefulness of an integrated framework based on meaning-making in examining similar experiences. In addition, investigating how different levels and kinds of challenges and support (either in gap year programs or in other experiential pedagogies) could help to further illuminate the possibilities for catalyzing changes in one's meaning-making.

Just as the literature on service learning has grown over the years, the literature on the gap year can move in a similar direction. As an early effort in this field, the level of analysis in this study was not extremely in-depth or focused on particular ways that participants report changing as a result of their experiences. However, with a foundational understanding of the main changes that volunteers frequently report from their gap year experiences, future work can begin to examine each of these, such as interpersonal changes, in greater depth.

Moreover, this study found that particular variables, challenges, and contextual influences were important for volunteers. In future work, research could begin to introduce some mixed-methods investigations and greater comparative dimensions to examine these influences. Investigations into how particular programmatic variables, such as country location, fundraising, project role and setting, duration, language training, forms of reflection, and overseas support that volunteers have before, during, and after the gap year would be helpful in assisting people gain more from their gap year experiences.

I limited my study to volunteers who were no more than four years out from their gap year. While this focus was illuminating, future research could include an older sample to explore influences over the life course. Moreover, further research on how these gap year volunteers perform in higher education and how they can best build upon their experiences and be supported in college would be helpful to practitioners in higher education. Similarly, this study identified some of the challenges that volunteers experienced returning home, and further research exploring these tensions seems warranted. In addition, longitudinal studies that follow one particular group, including spending time overseas with the volunteers, could be potentially helpful in exploring changes people experience as they occur and would illuminate the process of changing meaning-making in greater detail.

It would also be helpful to expand the range of locations and backgrounds of participants. For instance, as the gap year industry expands internationally, research with participants from other countries, such as the United States and Australia, would be beneficial. Research on domestic gap years, along with gap years taken at a different point in participants' lives (e.g., postcollege), would likewise be helpful to the field. The sample in this study was largely middle class, and it would also be interesting to conduct studies with more diverse groups of participants, in terms of socioeconomic background, ethnicity, and other variables. This study also found surprisingly high numbers of young people with mental health disorders who took a gap year, and understanding how these young people navigate through and are influenced by the gap year experience and different environments, both in the short and long term, would be useful.

Finally, as with much of the literature on the gap year and overseas volunteering, there is a dearth of investigations regarding how gap year volunteers influence the communities in which they are working, and future research should examine this important, and often overlooked, aspect of gap year experiences. As a whole, I hope that this study contributes to the debate surrounding gap years and provides fertile ground to build upon for those interested in gap years in the future.

The Role of Gap Years in Education

How do we measure the success or failure of an educational system? Increasingly, policy debates have come to understand the value of education in terms of economic competitiveness. According to this view, individuals have an interest in education because it will make them employable, and societies have an interest in education because it will make them prosper in the global economy.

There is surely some truth to that view: education *is* critical to economic growth. But we play many more roles in the world than simply that of employee. We are also neighbors, citizens, and friends. Higher education is uniquely positioned to prepare young people for these roles. Indeed, colleges and universities represent society's last mass effort to shape the virtues and trajectories of its young people. Gap years may augment that effort at character development in new and powerful ways.

Although gap years may further some of the purposes of universities, gap years are plainly not a substitute for higher education. Higher education offers unique opportunities to further develop the faculties of young people, guiding them to new experiences and new ways of understanding the world. Moreover, a recognition of the influence of experiential pedagogies such as the gap year should not detract from a commitment to the liberal arts and the humanities. Nevertheless, an international volunteering gap year may offer students benefits beyond those available in the classroom; as a result, it could also help them to take full advantage of their time in college. As this research suggests, an international volunteering gap year may provide some of the benefits often sought in holistic education—helping universities to form not just productive workers but citizens of character.

As the practice of the gap year grows, universities can do more to accommodate deferrals from participating students and help returned volunteers build upon the foundations of a gap year. This includes supporting the students as they return, helping them reflect on their experiences and to place them in an academic light, deepen students' understanding of topics related to their gap year by facilitating undergraduate research projects, and to continue to challenge students' assumptions about the world. They can also help to provide former gap year students with the opportunities to continue to promote and reflect on the behaviors that often gave them particular meaning during their year: contributing to the well-being of others.

Further, this study has illustrated the importance of extra-academic activity and informal cultural experiences in shaping young people, their values, and their self-conceptions. This is a lesson of relevance to the way universities should organize themselves and relate to their students as well, and I am hopeful that increased attention to the gap year might catalyze a renewed focus on these dimensions of education more generally. Not only should universities aim to facilitate gap-year-like experiences for their students (such as study abroad, international volunteering programs, and community volunteering), but they should also consider how their own institutions could manifest the qualities that make such experiences valuable. In effect, this could mean fostering student independence in college life, considering cultural diversity in arranging student accommodation, providing students with the opportunities to be active members of a community (e.g., in student governments and student unions), and offering more opportunities where young people are given responsibility and asked to care for others.

As I hope I have shown throughout this book, international volunteering gap years can help to promote development in a variety of ways, among them encouraging virtues and particular perspectives that support the formation of able citizens. The more "others-oriented" view of life and a more intimate, active sense of a community that can be facilitated by gap-year experiences are traits that researchers have identified as important elements of our well-being and our democracy (Bok 2010; Baumeister et al. in press).

Moving forward, a clear message from my research is that we should begin to consider gap years for their educational potential—not just to improve individual well-being but to facilitate civic development in "ways the world needs." While more research is needed to develop and evaluate these programs and their learning outcomes, anyone with an interest in how people learn and develop—be they parents, educators, policy-makers, or young people themselves—should be excited as the practice of taking a gap year becomes a trend in higher education.

References

Abes, Elisa S., Susan R. Jones, and Marylu K. McEwen. 2007. "Reconceptualizing the Model of Multiple Dimensions of Identity: The role of meaning-making capacity in the construction of multiple identities." *Journal of College Student Development 48* (1): 1–22.

Adler, Peter S. 1975. "The transitional experience: An alternative view of culture shock." *Journal of Humanistic Psychology* 15 (4): 13–23.

Ansell, Nicola. 2008. "Third World gap year projects: Youth transitions and the mediation of risk," *Environment and Planning D: Society and Space* 26 (2): 218–240.

Appiah, Kwame A. 2006. *Cosmopolitanism: Ethics in a world of strangers.* New York: Norton.

Arenson, Karen W. 2008. "Princeton to help students spend 'gap year' abroad." *The New York Times,* February 19.

Astin, Alexander W. 1984. "Student involvement: A developmental theory for higher education." *Journal of College Student Development* 40 (5): 518–529.

Bandura, Albert. 1986. *Social foundations of thought and action: A social cognitive theory.* Englewood Cliffs, NJ: Prentice Hall.

Barnett, Ronald. 2007. *A will to learn: Being a student in an age of uncertainty.* Maidenhead, Berkshire, UK: Open University Press.

Barrett, David. 2010. "Universities chief declares death of 'gap year' and proposes 'bridging year' instead." *The Telegraph,* August 15.

Battistoni, Richard M. 1985. *Public schooling and the education of democratic citizens.* Jackson: University Press of Mississippi.

Baumeister, Roy, Kathleen Vohs, Jennifer Aaker, and Emily Garbinsky. in press. "Some Key Differences between a Happy Life and a Meaningful Life." *Journal of Positive Psychology.*

Baxter Magolda, Marcia B. 1999a. *Creating contexts for learning and self-authorship: Constructive-developmental pedagogy.* Nashville, TN: Vanderbilt University Press.

Baxter Magolda, Marcia B. 1999b. "The evolution of epistemology: Refining contextual knowing at twentysomething." *Journal of College Student Development,* 40: 333–344.

Baxter Magolda, Marcia B. 2001. *Making their own way: Narratives for transforming higher education to promote self-development.* Sterling, VA: Stylus.

Baxter Magolda, Marcia B. 2009. "The activity of meaning-making: A holistic perspective on college student development." *Journal of College Student Development* 50 (6): 621–639.

Bennett, Milton J. 1993. Towards ethnorelativism: A developmental model of intercultural sensitivity. In *Education for the intercultural experience,* edited by R.M. Paige. Yarmouth, ME: Intercultural Press.

Birch, Elisa R., and Paul W. Miller. 2007. "The characteristics of 'gap year' students and their tertiary academic outcomes." *The Economic Record* 83 (262): 329–344.

Blackburn, George A., Gordon Clark, and David Pilgrim. 2005. "The gap year for geographers." *Geography* 90 (1): 32–41.

Boes, Lisa M., Marcia B. Baxter Magolda, and Jennifer A. Buckley. 2010. "Foundational assumptions and constructive-developmental theory." In *Development and assessment of self-authorship: Exploring the concept across cultures,* edited by Marcia B. Baxter Magolda, Elizabeth G. Creamer, and Peggy S. Meszaros, 3–24. Sterling, VA: Stylus Publishing.

Bohls, Elizabeth A., and Ian Duncan. 2005. *Travel writing 1700–1830: An anthology.* Oxford: Oxford University Press.

Bok, Derek. 2010. *The politics of happiness: What government can learn from the new research on well-being.* Princeton: Princeton University Press.

Brooks, Kate. 2002. "Talking about volunteering: A discourse analysis approach to volunteer motivations." *Voluntary Action* 4 (3): 13–30.

Buckles, Greg. 2013. "Thinking about a gap year? Read on . . ." http://www.middlebury.edu/admissions/apply/decisions/gapyearinfo

Chafin, Chris. 2012. "Freshman year, refreshed." http://www.newschool.edu/pressroom/press releases/2012/GlobalCitizenYear.htm.

Cheng, Kathy, and Robin Pendoley. 2012. "USA gap year fairs." http://www.usagapyearfairs.org.

Chickering, Arthur W., and Linda Reisser. 1993. *Education and identity,* 2nd ed. San Francisco: Jossey-Bass.

Clagett, Robert. 2011. "As Jan. 1 application deadline nears, an argument for a yearlong breather." *The Choice Blog,* December 27. http://thechoice.blogs.nytimes.com/2011/12/27/clagett-gap-year.

Cohen, Michele. 2001. "The Grand Tour: Language, national identity and masculinity." *Changing English* 8 (2): 129–141.

Crawford, Claire, and Jonathan Cribb. 2012. *Gap year takers: Uptake, trends and long term outcomes.* Research report number 252. United Kingdom Department for Education.

Crittenden, Jack. 2007. "Civic education." *The Stanford encyclopedia of philosophy,* edited by Edward N. Zalta. http://plato.stanford.edu/entries/civic-education.

Csikszentmihalyi, Mihaly, Reed Larson, and Suzanne Prescott. 1977. "The ecology of adolescent activity and experience." *Journal of Youth and Adolescence* 6 (3): 281–294.

Dalton, Jon C. 1988. "Men and leadership in college student personnel services." *New Directions for Student Services* 1988 (42): 79–89.

Delworth, Ursula, and David Seeman. 1984. "The ethics of care: Implications of Gilligan for the student services profession." *Journal of College Student Personnel* 25: 489–492.

Derryberry, W. Pitt, and Stephen J. Thoma. 2000. "The friendship effect: Its role in the development of moral thinking in students." *About Campus* 5 (2): 13–18.

Dewey, John. 1889/2001. "The school and society." *The school and society and the child and the curriculum.* Mineola, NY: Courier Dover Publications.

Dewey, John. 1916/1980. "The need of an industrial education in an industrial democracy." In *The middle works, 1899–1924,* edited by Jo Ann Boydston, 137–143. Carbondale: Southern Illinois University Press.

Dewey, John. 1938. *Experience and education.* New York: Collier/Macmillan.

Donahue, Teresa. 2009. "The making of global citizens through education abroad programs: Aligning missions and visions with education abroad programs." PhD diss., University of Southern California.

Evans, Alice F., Robert A. Evans, and William B. Kennedy. 1987. *Pedagogies of the non-poor.* Merryknoll, NY: Orbis Books.

Evans, Nancy J., Deanna S. Forney, Kristen A. Renn, Lori D. Patton, and Florence M. Guido. 2009. *Student development in college: Theory, research, and practice.* San Francisco: Jossey-Bass.

Eyler, Janet, and Dwight E. Giles Jr. 1999. *Where's the learning in service-learning?* San Francisco: Jossey Bass.

Freire, Paulo. 1970. *Pedagogy of the oppressed*. New York: Continuum.

Gilligan, Carol. 1982. *In a different voice: Psychological theory and women's development*. Cambridge, MA: Harvard University Press.

Gregory, Sean. 2010. "Time out: Gauging the value of a gap year before college." *Time*, September 21.

The Guardian. 2002. "Clarke appoints minister for gap years." *The Guardian*, December 4.

Hart, Mestiza. 2001. "Transforming boundaries of power in the classroom: Learning from La Mestiza." In *Power in practice*, edited by Ronald M. Cervero, Arthur L. Wilson, and Associates, 164–184. San Francisco: Jossey-Bass.

Harvard University. 2007. "Report of the Task Force on General Education." Task force on General Education, Faculty of Arts and Sciences. Cambridge, MA: Harvard University.

Heath, Sue. 2007. "Widening the gap: Pre-university gap years and the 'economy of experience.'" *British Journal of Sociology of Education* 28 (1): 89–103.

Helliwell, John, and Robert Putnam. 2004. The social context of well-being. *Philosophical Transactions Royal Society London B* (359): 1435–1446.

Howlett, Steven. 2004. "Volunteering and mental health: A literature review." *Voluntary Action* 6 (2): 55–72.

Hustinx, Lesley. 2001. "Individualisation and new styles of youth volunteering: An empirical exploration." *Voluntary Action* 3 (2): 57–76.

Ito, Fumihiko. 2011. "Universities seek to utilize gap years." *The Japan News*, December 23.

Jones, Andrew. 2004. *Review of gap year provision*. Research report number. 555. United Kingdom Department for Education and Skills.

Jones, Andrew. 2005. "Assessing international youth service programmes in two low income countries." *Voluntary Action* 7 (2): 87–100.

Jones, Susan R., and Elisa S. Abes. 2004. "Enduring influences of service-learning on college students' identity development." *Journal of College Student Development* 45 (2): 149–166.

Kahne, Joseph, and Joel Westheimer. 1999. "In the service of what? The politics of service-learning." In *Service-learning for youth empowerment and social change*, edited by Jeff Claus and Curtis Ogden, 25–38. New York: Peter Lang.

Kasser, Tim. 2002. *The high price of materialism*. Cambridge, MA: MIT Press.

Kauffmann, Norman, Judith N. Martin, Henry D. Weaver, and Judy Weaver. 1992. *Students abroad: Strangers at home*. Yarmouth, ME: Intercultural Press.

Kegan, Robert. 1982. *The evolving self: Problem and process in human development*. Cambridge, MA: Harvard University Press.

Kegan, Robert. 1994. *In over our heads: The mental demands of modern life*. Cambridge, MA: Harvard University Press.

Kellogg, Wendy. A. 1999. "Toward more transformative service-learning: Experiences from an urban environmental problem-solving class." *Michigan Journal of Community Service-learning* Fall: 63–73.

Kiely, Richard. 2002. "Toward an expanded conceptualization of transformational learning: A case study of international service-learning in Nicaragua." PhD diss., Cornell University.

Kiely, Richard. 2004. "A chameleon with a complex: Searching for transformation in international service-learning." *Michigan Journal of Community Service-learning* 10(2): 5–20.

Kim, Jim Y. 2010. Dartmouth University Presidential Lecture. http://www.dartmouth.edu/~president/pls/kim.html

Kim, Young Yun. 2001. *Becoming intercultural: An integrative theory of communication and cross-cultural adaptation*. Thousand Oaks, CA: Sage.

King, A. (2007) "A life changing experience"? A situated analysis of identity work in young people's accounts of their gap year. PhD diss., University of Surrey, United Kingdom.

King, Patricia M., and Marcia B. Baxter Magdola. 1996. "A developmental perspective on learning." *Journal of College Student Development* 37: 163–173.

Kleingeld, Pauline, and Eric Brown. 2006. "Cosmopolitanism." In *The Stanford encyclopedia of philosophy*, edited by Edward N. Zalta. http://plato.stanford.edu/entries/cosmopolitanism.

Kohlberg, Lawrence. 1981. *Essays on moral development*, vol. 1: *The philosophy of moral development: Moral stages and the idea of justice*. New York: Harper and Row.

Kristof, Nicholas. 2010. "Now grandma can 'win a trip' too." *The New York Times*, December 11.

Lambert, Victoria. 2010. "There is no cure for anorexia but now I want to get better." *The Telegraph*, May 10.

MacIntyre, Alasdair. 1981. *After virtue: A study in moral theory*. South Bend, IN: University of Notre Dame Press.

Martin, Andrew. 2010. "Should students have a gap year? Motivation and performance factors relevant to time out after completing school." *Journal of Educational Psychology 102* (3): 561–576.

McCauley, Cynthia D., Wilfred H. Drath, Charles J. Palus, Patricia M.G. O'Conner, and Becca A. Baker. 2006. "The use of constructive-developmental theory to advance the understanding of leadership." *The Leadership Quarterly* 17: 634–653.

McGuire, Jenifer, and Wendy C. Gamble. 2006. "Community service for youth: The value of psychological engagement over number of hours spent." *Journal of Adolescence* 29 (2): 289–298.

Mezirow, Jack. 2009. "Transformative learning theory." In *Transformative learning in practice: Insights from community, workplace, and higher education*, edited by Jack Mezirow, and Edward W. Taylor, 18–32. San Francisco: Jossey-Bass.

Mezirow, Jack, and Associates. 2000. *Learning as transformation: Critical perspectives on a theory in progress*, San Francisco: Jossey-Bass.

Mill, John Stuart. 1863/1972. *Utilitarianism, on liberty and considerations on representative government*. London: Everyman's Library/Dent.

Mitchell, David. 2011. "Gap-year travel may broaden the mind—but who needs a broad mind these days?" *The Guardian*, January 9.

The National Task Force on Civic Learning and Democratic Engagement. 2012. *A Crucible Moment: College Learning and Democracy's Future*. Washington, DC: Association of American Colleges and Universities.

Nicolaides, Aliki, and Lyle Yorks. 2007. An epistemology of learning through life. In *Explorations in complexity thinking*, edited by Kurt A. Richardson and Paul Cilliers, 223–235. Mansfield, MA: ISCE Publishing.

Nie, Norman H., Jane Junn, and Kenneth Stehlik-Barry. 1996. *Education and democratic citizenship in America*. Chicago: University Of Chicago Press.

Noddings, Nel. 1984. *Caring: A feminine approach to ethics and moral education*. Berkeley: University of California Press.

Nussbaum, Martha Cohen. 1996. "Cosmopolitanism and patriotism." In *For love of country: Debating the limits of patriotism*, edited by Martha Cohen Nussbaum and Joshua Cohen, 3–17. Boston: Beacon Press.

Nussbaum, Martha Cohen. 1997. *Cultivating humanity: A classical defense of reform in liberal education*. Cambridge, MA: Harvard University Press.

O'Shea, Joseph. 2010. "From Florida State to Oxford: Character, the Rhodes scholarship, and the gap year." *Journal of College and Character* 11 (2): 1–7.

O'Shea, Joseph. 2011. "A disposition for benevolence." *Journal of College and Character 12* (3): 1–4.

Pagano, Maria, Stephen G. Post, and Shannon M. Johnson. 2010. "Alcoholics Anonymous–related helping and the Helper Therapy Principle." *Alcoholism Treatment Quarterly* 29 (1): 23–34.

Pagano, Maria E., Brie B. Zeltner, Jihad Jaber, Stephen G. Post, William H. Zywiak, and Robert L. Stout. 2009. "Helping others and long-term sobriety: Who should I help to stay sober?" *Alcoholism Treatment Quarterly* 27 (1) 38–50.

Palmer, Parker. 1980. *The promise of paradox: A celebration of contradictions in the Christian life.* San Francisco: Jossey-Bass.

Palmer, Parker. 2010. "Toward a philosophy of integrative education." In *The heart of higher education: A call to renewal*, edited by Parker Palmer and Arthur Zajonc, 19–34. San Francisco, CA: Jossey-Bass.

Papastephanou, Marianna. 2002. "Arrows not yet fired: Cultivating cosmopolitanism through education." *Journal of Philosophy of Education* 36 (1): 69–86.

Parks, Sharon Daloz. 2000. *Big questions, worthy dreams: Mentoring young adults in their search for meaning, purpose, and faith.* San Francisco: Jossey-Bass.

Pascarella, Ernest T., and Patrick T. Terenzini. 2005. *How college affects students*, vol. 2: *A third decade of research.* San Francisco: Jossey-Bass.

Perry, William. 1970. *Forms of intellectual and ethical development in the college years: A scheme.* New York: Holt, Rinehart, and Winston.

Piaget, Jean. 1950. *The psychology of intelligence.* New York: Routledge.

Pizzolato, Jane Elizabeth. 2003. "Developing self-authorship: Exploring the experiences of high-risk college students." *Journal of College Student Development* 44 (6): 797–812.

Pizzolato, Jane Elizabeth. 2005. "Creating crossroads for self-authorship: Investigating the provocative moment." *Journal of College Student Development,* 46 (6): 624–641.

Pring, Richard. 2008. "Aims and values," Issues Paper 6. In *Nuffield Review of Education and Training.* www.nuffield14-19review.org.U.K.

Putnam, Robert. 2000. *Bowling alone.* New York: Simon and Schuster.

Pujol, Jesús, Pere Vendrell, Carme Junqué, Josep L. Martí-Vilalta, and Antoni Capdevila. 1993. "When does human brain development end? Evidence of corpus callosum growth up to adulthood." *Annals of Neurology* 34: 71–75.

Rhoads, Robert. 1997. *Community service and higher learning: Explorations of the caring self.* Albany, NY: SUNY Press.

Rhoads, Robert. 2000. "Democratic citizenship and service learning: Advancing the caring self." *New Directions for Teaching and Learning* 82: 37–44.

Rosero-Bixby, Luis, Andrea Collado, and Mitchell A. Seligson, "Social capital, urban settings and demographic behavior in Latin America." Paper presented at the IUSSP XXV International Population Conference, Tours, France, 2005.

Sanford, Nevitt. 1962. "Developmental status of the entering freshman." In *The American college: A psychological and social interpretation of the higher learning*, edited by Nevitt Sanford, 253–282. New York: Wiley and Sons.

Serow, Robert. 1991. "Students and voluntarism: Looking into the motives of community service participants." *American Educational Research Journal* 28 (3): 543–556.

Shkedi, Asher. 2004. "Second-order theoretical analysis: A method for constructing theoretical explanation." *International Journal of Qualitative Studies in Education* 17 (5): 627–646.

Siegel, Daniel. 2010. *Mindsight: The new science of personal transformation.* New York: Bantam Books.

Simpson, Kate. 2004. "'Doing development': The gap year, volunteer-tourists and popular practice of development." *Journal of International Development* 16: 681–692.

Smith, Adam. 1776/1976. "An inquiry into the nature and causes of the wealth of nations." In *The Glasgow edition of the works and correspondence of Adam Smith*, vol. 2, edited by Roy Harold Campbell and Andrew S. Skinner. Oxford: Clarendon Press.

Sparrow, Lise. 2000. "Beyond multicultural man: Complexities of identity." *International Journal of Intercultural Relations* 24 (2): 173–201.

Suh, Esther Kang. 2009. "Helping across continents: A holistic understanding of six undergraduate students' experiences as international volunteers." PhD diss., Columbia University.

Tanner, Jennifer L., Jeffrey Jensen Arnett, and Julie A. Leis. 2008. "Emerging adulthood: Learning and development during the first stage of adulthood." In *Handbook of research on adult learning and development*, edited by M. Cecil Smith and Nancy DeFrates-Densch, 34–67. New York: Routledge.

Taylor, Edward. 1993. "A learning model of becoming interculturally competent. A transformative process." PhD diss., University of Georgia.

Taylor, Edward. 1994. "Intercultural competency: A transformative learning process." *Adult Education Quarterly* 44 (3): 154–174.

Tisdell, Elizabeth. 2001. "The politics of positionality: Teaching for social change in higher education." In *Power in practice*, edited by Ronald M. Cervero, Arthur L. Wilson, and Associates, 145–163. San Francisco: Jossey-Bass.

Todd, Sharon. "Facing humanity: The difficult task of cosmopolitan education." Paper presented at the Annual Conference of the Philosophy of Education Society of Great Britain, Oxford, United Kingdom, March, 2008.

Uehara, Asako. 1986. "The nature of American student re-entry adjustment and perceptions of the sojourn experience." *International Journal of Intercultural Relations* 10 (4): 415–438.

Universities and Colleges Admissions Service. 2006. Media release. http://www.ucas.ac.U.K./about_us/media_enquiries/media_releases/2006/2006-10-18

Unstead-Joss, Ruth. 2008. "An analysis of volunteer motivation: Implications for international development." *The Journal of the Institute for Volunteering Research Volume* 9 (1): 3–20.

Welikala, Thushari, and Chris Watkins. 2008. *Improving intercultural learning experiences in higher education: Responding to cultural scripts for learning*. London: University of London.

White, Robert. W., 1981. "Humanitarian concern." In *The modern American college*, edited by Arthur W. Chickering and Associates, 158–171. San Francisco: Jossey-Bass.

Wilson, John, and Marc Musick. 1999. "The effects of volunteering on the volunteer." *Law and Contemporary Problems* 62 (4): 141–168.

Yeung, Anne Birgitta. 2004. "The Octagon Model of volunteer motivation: Results of a phenomenological analysis." *Voluntas* 15: 21–46.

Zajonc, Arthur. 2010. "Experience, contemplation, and transformation." In *The heart of higher education: A call to renewal*, edited by Parker J. Palmer and Arthur Zajonc, 101–124. San Francisco: Jossey-Bass.

Zurcher, Louis. A., 1978: "Ephemeral roles, voluntary action, and voluntary associations." *Journal of Voluntary Action Research* 7: 65–74.

Index

Joseph O'Shea serves as director of undergraduate research at Florida State University, where he also received his bachelor's degree in philosophy and social science. A Truman and Rhodes Scholar, he has a master's degree in comparative social policy and a Ph.D. in education from the University of Oxford. Dr. O'Shea has been involved with developing education and health-care initiatives in communities in the United States and sub-Saharan Africa. Translating his research into practice, he also developed FSU's Global Scholars Program, which places students in volunteer, intern, and research roles in developing countries around the world.